6x 2/02 11/04
9 x 4/10-2/11

OVERLAND WITH KIT CARSON

WITHDRAWN

DEC 1994

Col G D Brereton

OVERLAND
WITH KIT CARSON

A NARRATIVE OF
The Old Spanish Trail in '48

by
GEORGE DOUGLAS BREWERTON

Containing Many Illustrations in Line
BY THE AUTHOR

WITH AN INTRODUCTION
AND ORIGINAL MAP

by
STALLO VINTON

*Introduction to the Bison Book Edition
by Marc Simmons*

University of Nebraska Press
Lincoln and London

████████████████

Introduction to the Bison Book Edition copyright © 1993 by
the University of Nebraska Press
All rights reserved
Manufactured in the United States of America

First Bison Book printing: 1993
Most recent printing indicated by the last digit below:
10   9   8   7   6   5   4   3   2   1

Library of Congress Cataloging-in-Publication Data
Brewerton, George Douglas, 1820–1901.
Overland with Kit Carson: a narrative of the old Spanish trail in
'48 / by George Douglas Brewerton; containing many illustrations in line by the author with an introduction and original
map by Stallo Vinton.—Bison Book ed.
p.
Includes bibliographical references and index.
ISBN 0-8032-6113-6
1. Southwest, New—Description and travel.   2. Carson, Kit,
1809–1868.   3. Brewerton, George Douglas, 1820–1901.
4. Mormon Trail.   I. Carson, Kit, 1809–1868.   II. Title.
F786.B84   1993   93-10688
979—dc20   CIP

Reprinted from the original edition published in 1930 by
Coward-McCann, Inc., New York

∞

Acknowledgment is due to Miss Mabel Malbone Brewerton, daughter of George Douglas Brewerton, for biographical data and for the portrait of her father which is the frontispiece of this volume. Thanks are also extended to Frederick S. Dellenbaugh, Esq., for his aid in my determination of the Old Spanish Trail.

CONTENTS

MAP OF THE OLD SPANISH TRAIL AND THE
SANTA FE TRAIL . . . . x–xiii
INTRODUCTION TO THE BISON BOOK EDITION . . xv
INTRODUCTION 3
The Old Spanish Trail——The News of the
Gold Discovery.
SKETCH OF LIFE OF GEORGE DOUGLAS BREWER-
TON 23

A RIDE WITH KIT CARSON

I. FROM LOS ANGELES TO THE MOJAVE . . . 31
By ship from San Francisco——Arrival at
San Pedro——Journey to Los Angeles——
Description of Pueblo de Los Angeles——
Arrival of Carson——Camp at Bridge Creek
——Preparations for journey——The start
——The order of march——The last house
——The Cajon Pass.

II. FROM THE MOJAVE TO THE ARCHILETTE . . 53
On the desert——A recalcitrant mule——On
the Old Spanish Trail——The Mexican cara-
van——A drink à la Byron——Discipline
for Juan——A rattlesnake for bed-fellow
——Passage over the desert——Carson's
watchfulness——Jornado del Muerto——
Bill Williams' horse-stealing expedition——
Lost on the desert——Saved by the mule——
Meeting with Indians——Meeting with Jo-
seph Walker——The pipe of peace——
Habits of Digger Indians——A sneak thief
——Signal smoke——The hostage.

III. FROM THE ARCHILETTE TO LITTLE SALT LAKE . 87
Fuentes and Hernandez——Revenge of Carson and Godey——Arrival at the Rio Virgen——Scene of Tabeau's death——Archambeau shoots a Digger——Las Vegas de
Santa Clara.

vii

IV. From Little Salt Lake to the Grand River 100
Meeting with Eutaws——Wacarra——An
Indian trencherman——And a skillful horse-
trader——A gift to Wacarra's squaw——
Over the Wah-Satch——Mules first experi-
ence with snow——Camping in the snow——
Fishing with arrows and with sticks——
Fate of the seven Arkansaw travellers——
Crossing Grand River——The raft——The
upset——Loss of arms and provisions.

V. From the Grand River to Taos . . . 123
Short rations——Horse flesh——Failure of
negotiations for a puppy——A deer hunt
with Carson——Over the Divide to Taos
Valley——Indian sign——Mexican traders
——Encounter with Indians——A tense
situation——Carson's defiance——Retirement of the enemy——The first settlement
——Arrival at Taos——Carson's wife.

Incidents of Travel in New Mexico

VI. From Taos to Santa Fé 147
Description of Taos——Carson remains at
Taos——A shot from the brush——Way-
side crosses——Camp at a village——Father
Ignatio——And his party——The Alcalde's
hospitality——The wrong path——The
wood cutters——Steering gear for a burro
——Arrival at Santa Fé.

VII. At Santa Fé 177
The United States Hotel——A gambling sa-
loon——Lady Tules——The priest——A
custom of the country——Navajo Indians
——Arrival of Carson——A change of plan
——Departure of Carson.

VIII. From Santa Fé to the Mora 201
Arrangements with a wagon train——Ruins
at the Pecos——The eternal fire——The

Fourth of July——Whirlwinds and mirages
——Arrival at the Mora——A railroad to
the Pacific.

IN THE BUFFALO COUNTRY

IX. FROM THE MORA TO THE PAWNEE FORK . . 219
The wagon train——The Great Prairies——
Method of the march——Fight between Eu-
taws and Comanches——A ghastly target
——To the top of Round Mound——The
first buffalo hunt——A thunderstorm on the
Cimarron——A stampede of buffaloes——A
night march——The Arkansas crossing——
Meeting with Aubry——Aubry's ride.

X. FROM THE PAWNEE FORK TO INDEPENDENCE . 260
Delayed by a flood——Dead buffaloes——
Description of the Prairies——Another buffalo hunt——The Indians take a hand——A
narrow escape——A dash ahead of the caravan——Arrival at Independence——Death
of Old Bill Williams.

NOTES 289
BIBLIOGRAPHY 293
INDEX 297

THE OLD SPANISH TRAIL
AND
THE SANTA FÉ TRAIL

Route of Brewerton   thus ·······
Alternative Routes   thus ─────
Route of Carson after
leaving Brewerton   thus ++++

As determined by
STALLO VINTON
for
OVERLAND WITH KIT CARSON

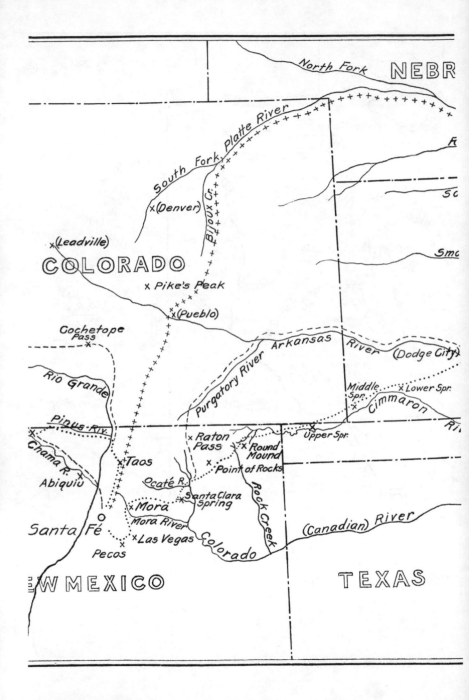

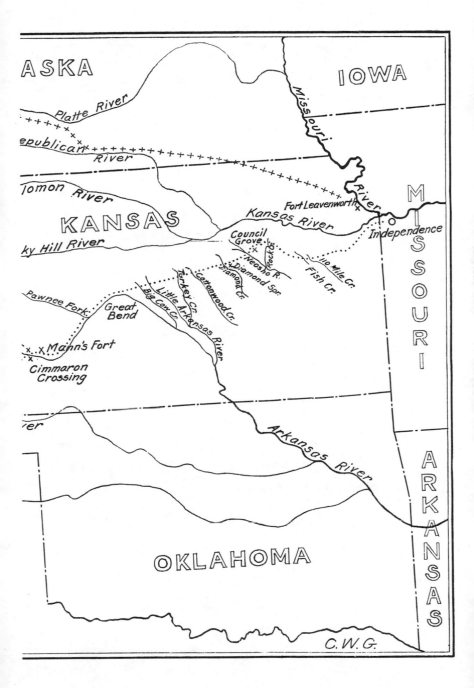

INTRODUCTION TO THE BISON BOOK EDITION

By Marc Simmons

When famed mountain man, scout, and government courier Christopher "Kit" Carson left Los Angeles in early May of 1848 to carry official dispatches to Washington, the Mexican War, which added California to the Union, had only recently ended, and gold had just been discovered at Sutter's Mill. It was a stirring time in the history of the country, and Carson was one of those who played a significant and memorable role in the unfolding of events west of the Mississippi.

We can be grateful that in the party accompanying Carson on his long-distance ride was a young army lieutenant, George Douglas Brewerton, a keen observer who in the following decade would publish a lively account of the experience. Brewerton, at age nineteen, had enlisted on the East Coast in the First Regiment of New York Volunteers and with the unit had been sent by ship on a six-month voyage around the Horn of South America to California. From their arrival at San Francisco Bay in March of 1847, Lt. Brewerton and his fellow volunteers served routine garrison duty over the succeeding year, acting in effect as an army of occupation.

By the spring of 1848, with the Mexican War concluded, it appeared that the regiment would soon be disbanded, so Brewerton obtained a transfer to the first United States Infantry. His new duty station was three-quarters way across the continent in Mississippi and to get there the military governor of California, Colonel Richard B. Mason, ordered him to accompany Kit Carson on the dispatch mission, at least as far as Missouri where Brewerton could then turn south. These were the circumstances that launched the youthful lieutenant on his adventurous ride and furnished him the opportunity to make a small but notable contribution to the history of the American West.

Kit Carson, for his part, had come out to California (1845) in the company of the pathfinder John Charles Frémont and participated in the Bear Flag Revolt, an armed movement that set the stage for the acquisition of that Mexican province by the United States. On September 5, 1846, Carson was ordered to ride to Washington with news of the military situation on the West Coast, a task Frémont described as "service of high trust and honor, but of great danger also."

On this, the first of three courier trips Kit would make from west to east, he followed the southern route, generally called the Gila Trail, leading across the lower portions of California and Arizona to a link-up with the Santa Fe Trail in New Mexico. On this journey, however, he was stopped at the Rio Grande near Socorro, New Mexico, by General Stephen Watts Kearny, who was marching west with soldiers to complete the conquest of California and needed Carson's services as a guide. The dispatches were carried to

Washington by another, and Kit faced about and retraced the trail he had just ridden over.

The following March, 1847, he was again commissioned to be the bearer of dispatches to the War Department and he departed California with a brilliant young naval officer, Lieutenant Edward F. Beale, as his companion. After surviving an Indian attack on the Gila Trail and ascending the Santa Fe Trail to Fort Leavenworth, the pair continued on to Washington by riverboat and train, arriving there in May.

A few weeks later, Carson returned to California, again transporting pouches of government mail. The winter of 1847–48 he spent guarding Cajon Pass east of Los Angeles to intercept Indians fleeing with stolen livestock. It was the following May that he received orders from Col. Mason to undertake one last transcontinental ride in the service of his country. Numbered among the twenty-seven men of his escort company was the novice, Lieutenant Brewerton.

On this occasion, Kit elected to take not the Gila Trail of his previous trips but rather a route farther to the north called the Old Spanish Trail. This little-known pathway had its origins in 1776 when two priests, Fathers Atanasio Domínguez and Silvestre Vélez de Escalante, departing Santa Fe, attempted to blaze a connecting trail to Spanish California. Early winter snows in western Utah forced their expedition to turn back, however, and for the remainder of the colonial period New Mexico and California remained unjoined. Finally in 1829, a native New Mexican, Antonio Armijo, led a small trading expedition over portions of the path pioneered earlier by Domínguez and Escalante and went on to reach southern California, thereby definitively opening the Old Spanish Trail to commercial traffic at a time when the Republic of Mexico held title to the land.

The trail, as traveled by Carson and Brewerton in 1848, stretched some 1,200 miles in a giant parabola, crossing California's Mojave Desert and the tip of the future state of Nevada, and then arching northward into central Utah before dropping down through Colorado and traversing the New Mexico boundary to arrive at last in Santa Fe. Owing to the ruggedness of the terrain, the trail was passable only with packtrains of mules, not wagons. The inexperienced Lt. Brewerton found its passage filled with unrelieved hardship and peril.

In his memoirs, dictated in 1856 while he was serving as Indian agent in New Mexico, Kit Carson summarized his last courier mission over the Old Spanish Trail in two brief paragraphs.* Fortunately for us, much else of interest that occurred on that trip and which he neglected to record was set down by Brewerton in his lengthy account. Indeed, the lieutenant's narrative is our only full and detailed description left by any traveler on the Old Spanish Trail.

George Brewerton performed another service as

---

*Carson's memoirs, edited by Milo Milton Quaife, have been reprinted as a Bison Book under the title *Kit Carson's Autobiography* by the University of Nebraska Press, Lincoln.

well in drawing an authentic portrait of one of the nation's most celebrated folk heroes. "The *real* Kit Carson I found to be a plain, simple, unostentatious man," he wrote. "[He] was one of Dame Nature's gentlemen—a sort of article which she gets up occasionally, but nowhere in better style than among the backwoods of America." Under the stress of a wilderness journey, men display their true character and Kit's performance as guide and leader earned the admiration of his youthful companion. Brewerton learned much from the trailwise Carson about survival, the nature of the country, and the ways of Indians. His positive view of the man, based on firsthand observations, is useful to recall these days when Kit Carson is so often depicted in popular literature as a man of low character and a rabid Indian hater.

The circumstances that led to the writing and publication of the Brewerton account are these: In the course of his overland journey, the lieutenant kept no diary, but rather made notes and prepared artistic sketches of scenes along the route. These materials, however, were lost midway through the trip when a raft being used to ford a Utah river capsized. Thus, five years later when he had the opportunity to write up his experiences for *Harper's New Monthly Magazine,* a widely read periodical of the day, Brewerton was obliged to depend wholly upon memory. Luckily, being young, his recollection was sharp and he was able to give a vivid recital of the stirring adventures that befell him in 1848.

Harper's published the narrative serially, in three long installments. The first (August 1853) appeared under the title "A Ride with Kit Carson through the Great American Desert and the Rocky Mountains." It began with the dispatch party's departure from Los Angeles and ended with its arrival in Taos, where Kit had his home and wife (Josepha Jaramillo), whom Brewerton termed an amiable Spanish lady. In this section, the lieutenant recounts in some detail the company's harrowing experience about fifty miles north of Taos when, travel-weary and almost out of ammunition, it unexpectedly bumped into a hostile camp of Utes and Apaches. Kit's memoirs explain the episode in four meager sentences. But luckily Brewerton fleshes out the full story, coming to the conclusion that in the crisis only Carson's boldness saved the lives of the party.

Harper's second installment (April 1854) was entitled "Incidents of Travel in New Mexico." Shortest of the three, it contains the author's observations on Taos society, a commentary on the singular experiences encountered on a four-day trip south to Santa Fe, and a candid portrayal of life in the freewheeling New Mexican capital. Coming from California through all kinds of weather and living on short rations for almost six weeks, Brewerton had remained in good health. But strangely now, while in Santa Fe and sleeping in a drafty room at the inn, he fell victim to an attack of influenza. That bit of misfortune worked a change in his travel plans and forced a premature leave-taking with Kit Carson.

It seems Carson had remained behind in Taos to spend a few extra days with his wife, but he appeared in Santa Fe on June 19, 1948, and delivered a communication from California's Col. Mason to Colonel Edward W. B. Newby, military commandant of the city. He also acquired fresh horses from the local quartermaster and with a scaled-down escort prepared to set forth on the final half of his cross-country ride. Confined to his sickbed, Lt. Brewerton sadly made his final goodbyes to Kit and the other members of the party. From that point forward, he was on his own.

Although Brewerton makes no further reference to the progress of Carson's mission, a word as to its outcome is in order here. Having heard that Indians were troublesome on the Santa Fe Trail leading directly back to Missouri, Kit chose to bypass the danger zone and take an out-of-the-way route that led northward through Colorado to the Platte River. Descending that stream by way of the Oregon Trail to Fort Kearney, Nebraska, he then angled across country, southeastward, to Fort Leavenworth. At the nearby river port of Weston, Missouri, Kit with his treasured dispatch pouches boarded the steamboat *St. Joseph* on July 25, and the last day of the month he landed in St. Louis, where rumors of his death at the hands of Indians had preceded him. Departing the next day, he was in Washington by August 4, exactly three months after he and George Brewerton had started from Los Angeles.

Meanwhile back in Santa Fe, Lt. Brewerton had recovered from his influenza and had arranged to con-

tinue east with a merchant train plying the Santa Fe
Trail. Its one hundred wagons rendered the caravan
safe from attack, although the lieutenant narrowly
escaped death at the hands of Comanches when in
central Kansas he left the train to hunt alone. The
chronicle of his journey over the trail to Independence, Missouri, formed the third installment in *Harper's* under the title "In the Buffalo Country." But its
publication was delayed until September of 1862,
owing to a fire in the magazine's publishing house
and temporary loss of the manuscript.

George Brewerton's articles remained buried in
the back files of *Harper's,* generally unknown to
scholars, until 1930 when they were resurrected, edited, and published for the first time in book form by
Stallo Vinton under the new title *Overland with Kit
Carson.* * Included in the introductory material was a
"Sketch of the Life of George Douglas Brewerton," the
facts furnished largely by his daughter. This piece remains the best source of biographical information on
the man in the years before and after his 1848 narrative.

The origin of the illustrations that first appeared in
the *Harper's* articles and were reproduced in *Overland with Kit Carson* requires comment. Author
Brewerton was also an accomplished landscape artist. In the original articles, his signature appeared
on eleven of the illustrations, while others seemed to

---

*The articles were published in book form again in 1969—in three lim-
ited edition volumes in buckram by Lewis Osborne, Ashland, Oregon.

be his work, although unsigned. From his sketches, the magazine's engravers prepared woodcuts for publication. In addition, they borrowed from the work of western artists Richard Kern and John Mix Stanley and used a plate initially published in Josiah Gregg's *Commerce of the Prairies* (1844). Not all of the art used by *Harper's* found its way into Stallo Vinton's book.

Finally, a word ought to be said concerning the attitudes toward other ethnic groups expressed in *Overland with Kit Carson.* Some of Brewerton's negative remarks about Indians and Mexicans, while considered offensive and unacceptable today, nevertheless must be understood in the context of the times.

In the aftermath of the Mexican War, anti-Catholic and anti-Mexican sentiment was rife throughout the United States. Brewerton, as an impressionable young soldier, could hardly have escaped its influence or failed to let it color opinions given in his writings. Notwithstanding, a close reading of him reveals that his criticism of others was based on their observed behavior, and he was as quick to condemn failings among his own kind as among the alien peoples he encountered for the first time in the far Southwest.

In sum, George D. Brewerton offers us a gripping account of personal adventure, one that occurred in an era that now seems quite remote and exotic to most Americans. In this single effort, the author left a lasting mark on the history of our frontier.

OVERLAND WITH KIT CARSON

INTRODUCTION

DURING the Mexican War, Brewerton, a boy of nineteen, eager and versatile, had gone to California by sailing vessel as a second lieutenant in the Stevenson Regiment of New York Volunteers. He returned overland from Los Angeles to Independence, Missouri, by the Old Spanish Trail and the Santa Fé Trail, and made the journey as far as Taos in company with the famous Kit Carson. The expedition left Los Angeles on the 4th of May, 1848, and for Brewerton the journey was to continue until his arrival in Independence during the month of August. His experiences are embodied in the present narrative, which first appeared in the pages of *Harper's New Monthly Magazine,* with illustrations mostly by his own hand.

The long threatened war with Mexico had become inevitable upon the admission of Texas to the Union. The seizure of the outlying possessions of our southern neighbor was planned far in advance of the opening of hostilities. The expeditions of Frémont during the previous four years were evidently made in the interest of military preparedness, for a large part of his exploration was in Alta California, which extended from the coast to the Rocky Mountains and was then Mexican territory.

It seems more than a coincidence, then, that Frémont was still in California when the war began. Always bold and supremely self-confident, he apparently exceeded his instructions, for even before he knew war was declared, and almost single-handed, he attempted the conquest of the country,—and came strangely near success until he ran foul of superior authority.

Coastal California was then very sparsely settled, a few thousand whites constituting all the non-Indian population. They mostly lived near the former missions and at the ports, which were mere villages, infrequently visited by whalers and the ships of West Coast fur traders. To the eastward, the land was totally uninhabited by white men to the distant settlements of Taos and Santa Fé, and in between were vast arid mountain and desert regions. True, much of the area had been traversed by the Franciscan missionary fathers and by such traders as Jedediah Smith, Wolfskill, Ogden and Joseph Walker, and recently by Frémont himself, but the result of these journeys was not yet generally available.

THE OLD SPANISH TRAIL

At the time of Brewerton's ride, the northern route to California, which later became the usual way to the gold fields because it was more direct, had been but little used. It left the Oregon Trail near Fort Bridger and went across what is now northern Nevada. There was another route which led from Santa Fé to southern California by way of the Gila River through the present Arizona. This had been the path of Kearny's little army in its invasion of California.

There was a third trail, also starting at Santa Fé, which took its course through central Utah, then south-west over the Mojave Desert, through the coastal mountains to Los Angeles. This was the Old Spanish Trail, or Great Spanish Trail, and was the path followed by Brewerton.

Two Franciscan fathers, burning with missionary zeal, were the first white men to set foot on any part of the Spanish Trail, except of course near the very extremities of San Gabriel and Taos. Father Francisco Garces, in his entrada of 1775-1776, penetrated to the Mojave Desert. Father Escalante in 1776 attempted a northern overland journey to the coast. He went from Santa Fé by the Chama, and the head waters of the San Juan and Dolores Rivers to the Grand River in Utah, crossed the Green, proceeded to Utah Lake, south to the Virgin and the Colorado. Here the westward trip was abandoned and the party made its way back, following the Colorado to the Crossing of the Fathers, thence up the San Juan and down the Chama and back to Santa Fé. Thus the Franciscans between them covered most of the trail, except the part that lies from the Virgin to the Mojave Rivers.

At the end of the first decade of the last century, American fur trappers commenced to penetrate the Rocky Mountains, and within a few years the upper waters of the Green River were well known to them, and ventures were made further and further into the wilderness. In 1826, Jedediah Smith went south from Salt Lake past Utah Lake to the Mojave Desert. Instead of crossing the mountains to the San Gabriel Mission, he turned north to the San Joaquin River.

Apparently the first white man to traverse the full length of the Spanish Trail was William Wolfskill, a Kentuckian, who in 1830-1831 made a journey leading a company of New Mexican traders. They set out from Santa Fé with packs of serapes and other woven fabrics for trade with the Indians. Business being poor, they boldly pushed on over

mountain and desert all the way to the coast. Their
wares brought tremendous prices in trade for horses,
mules and Chinese silks, all of which gave them
another profit on the second turnover cn their return. From then on, annual caravans made the
journey. The later traders must have degenerated
from the first bold spirits, for Irving B. Richman
states that they proved more expert as horse thieves
than as traders. As will be seen, Brewerton, who
overtook one of their trains, speaks contemptuously
of them.

Wolfskill, weary perhaps of the arid deserts of
New Mexico and the hardships of the mountains,
decided to stay in California. He settled on a ranch
near San Gabriel, where he established the large
vineyard and orchards which are considered the
founding of the fruit industry on the coast.

The Old Spanish Trail led from Los Angeles past
the San Gabriel Mission to the Cajon Pass between
the San Gabriel and San Bernardino Mountains,
and thence into the Mojave Desert. Leaving California it passed across the lower end of Nevada to
the Virgin River, and up the Virgin, crossing it
many times. In Utah, the trail passed over the
Beaver Dam Range to Las Vegas de Santa Clara
(later known as Mountain Meadows, the scene of
the great massacre of immigrants in 1857), and on
to Little Salt Lake.

Here begin variants in the trail, depending on different crossing of the Wasatch Mountains. An examination of the map will show the Sevier River flowing to the north from its sources in southern Utah, then turning west in a wide sweep and finally flowing south to its salt sink, Sevier Lake. To the east of Sevier River, in turn from south to north lie the Panguitch Mountains, the Awaga Plateau, and the Fish Lake and Wasatch Mountains. These are really part of one great chain and form the divide between the land-locked Interior Basin and the watershed of the Colorado. On the opposite side of the river are the Parowan, Tushar, and Pavant Mountains.

From Little Salt Lake a trail went almost due north to Utah Lake and Great Salt Lake. This was the course of Frémont and Carson in 1844. At various places, by the early fifties at least, paths branched off to the east to take advantage of passes in the mountains, all leading ultimately to Gunnison Valley. These trails began respectively at about the present towns of Parowan, Beaver and Nephi. To reach the crossing of the Green, the trail went to present Castle Dale either from the site of Salina through Wasatch Pass between the Fish Lake and Wasatch Ranges, or from the present Ephraim or Nephi directly, through the Wasatch Mountains proper. There was a route from Utah Lake up

Spanish Fork and down the Price River, which is now used by the Denver & Rio Grande Railroad.

A careful examination of the old maps and authorities has convinced the writer that Brewerton took the most southerly of the possible courses, and that this was the original Spanish Trail. It is true that Chittenden, in the fine map in his *American Fur Trade,* shows the Spanish Trail as going north from Little Salt Lake to a point which would be at about the present Fillmore. But the better view seems to be that it turned to the east at Little Salt Lake near the present Parowan. Frémont shows this most distinctly, for he says in his 1844 *Report,* p. 271, that the lake is nearly opposite a gap in the Wasatch chain through which the Spanish Trail passes. He further states that after four hundred and forty miles on the trail, on leaving Little Salt Lake he was compelled to explore a way through the wilderness, for the Spanish Trail bore off to the south-east, crossing the Wasatch, while his course led to the north-east, along the foot of the range. This determination of the trail is supported by the *Report* and map of the Beckwith (Gunnison) Expedition. Frémont must have based his statement on the physical path and on what he was told by Carson, who had been over the trail before. It was the shortest and most direct route, and was the one he and Brewerton would naturally follow, since they bore dispatches and were in a hurry. It seems fairly certain that the more northerly paths through the Wasatch Range did not come into use until a slightly later time, when the Mormons made their settlements all through this region and a network of roads linked their towns.

The Spanish Trail accordingly went from Little Salt Lake easterly between the Parowan and Tushar Mountains to Bear Creek and the Sevier River, north along the Sevier to Salina (Salado) Creek, up the Salina to Wasatch Pass at its headwaters, thence across Quitchupah, Muddy, Ferron and Cottonwood Creeks to Castle Dale on the San Rafael.

From Castle Dale the trail followed down the San Rafael River for some distance, then went more directly east to Gunnison Valley, where it crossed Green River near the mouth of the Price River.

From Gunnison Valley the trail led south-easterly to the crossing of the Grand at present Moab, up Spanish Valley, thence to the Rio Dolores, which was followed to its headwaters at the Continental Divide near the present Durango, Colorado.

Thence the trail went down the eastern slopes of the Rocky Mountains to the Chama, which has its source close to the boundary between Colorado and New Mexico, down the Chama past the ancient town of Abiquiu, to the Rio Grande and to Santa Fé.

There was an alternative route from Gunnison

Valley to the mouth of the Gunnison River, up that
river and the Uncompahgre, crossing the Continental
Divide by Cochetope Pass, and reaching the headwaters of the Rio Grande at San Luis Valley in
Colorado. Carson had used this path in part on a
trapping expedition to the Uinta, made in 1832 or
1833 and referred to by him on p. 30 of *Kit Carson's
Own Story.*

It is difficult to reconstruct Brewerton's path
through Utah and Colorado, since his narrative is
singularly barren of geographical details on this
part of the journey. The Wasatch Mountains, Trout
Lake, the Green and Grand Rivers (which two he
confuses), and the Continental Divide are the only
features he mentions at all. On June 3rd he arrived
at the Green River, and two days later crossed the
Grand. The only crossings of these rivers close
enough to be within two days travel by pack train
are at Gunnison Valley and Moab. So he must
have gone by the regular Spanish Trail, which again
is the shortest route.

The body of water Brewerton calls Trout Lake
cannot be identified. He refers to it as being in the
Wasatch Mountains, which to him probably meant
all the ranges east of the Sevier River. Both Panguitch Lake and Fish Lake seem too large to fit the
reference, and neither is close to what must have
been his course. In fact there are no lakes shown

on any maps of the region that in any way fit into the puzzle. Perhaps, through erosion of the rim of the outlet, the lake has ceased to exist.

Since Carson wished to go to Taos, where his family lived, he and Brewerton must have turned off from the trail somewhere about the boundary between Colorado and New Mexico. Instead of following down the Chama past Abiquiu to Santa Fé, they probably went from Monero to the headwaters of Pinos Creek and down it to the Rio Grande and Taos.

From Santa Fé, Brewerton traveled the well-known and clearly defined Santa Fé Trail, which requires no comment here, except the statement that he went by the more nearly direct Cimarron Route.

THE NEWS OF THE GOLD DISCOVERY

A CAREFUL analysis of all the available facts and circumstances demonstrates that on the journey of the text Carson and Brewerton brought with them to the East the first news of the momentous discovery of gold at Sutter's Mill.

It may seem remarkable that for months items as to the existence of gold in California appeared in the Eastern newspapers before any particular interest was aroused. Yet such is the fact. The great explosion of excitement can be definitely traced to the Message of President Polk to Congress in December, 1848. From then on it was the one topic, and thousands prepared for the rush which started with the opening of spring.

But the history of the gold fever in the East merely duplicated that in the West. Although gold had long previously been known to exist, the vital and significant discovery was made on the 24th day of January, 1848. Intelligence of it filtered into San Francisco, and samples were shown; and the news was published there in the *Californian* on the 15th of March, 1848. The announcement read as follows:

13

"Gold Mine Found.—In the newly made raceway of the Saw Mill recently erected by Captain Sutter, on the American Fork, gold has been found in considerable quantities. One person brought thirty dollars' worth to New Helvetia, gathered there in a short time. California, no doubt, is rich in mineral wealth, great chances here for scientific capitalists. Gold has been found in almost every part of the country.''

But it was only in May, even in San Francisco, that the frenzy started which caused a rush to the gold fields so universal that as Captain Folsom reported, ''Two or three merchants and a few soldiers constituted the entire population.''

To a member of the Stevenson Regiment belongs the honor of the first announcement in the East. His letter, dated San Francisco, April 1st, 1848, and addressed to the New York *Herald,* filled two columns of that paper on the 19th day of August following. It is unsigned and its authorship has not been traced.

Most of the letter is taken up with an account of the trip around the Horn, the military situation and agricultural and mercantile prospects. Sutter's ranch at New Helvetia is given special praise for a large crop of grain; although by the time he appears in print, the worthy Swiss, through some error in deciphering the penmanship of the letter-writer, is masquerading as ''M. Luther van Helvetia.''

The letter goes on to speak of:

"The mines of gold, silver, quicksilver, saltpeter, coal, &c&c which abound in these districts . . . I am credibly informed that a quantity of gold, worth in value $30 was picked up lately in the bed of a stream of the Sacramento. . . . The gold mine discovered in December last on the south branch of the American fork, in a range of low hills forming the base of the Sierra Nevada distant thirty miles from New Helvetia, is only three feet below the surface, in a strata of soft sand rock.   From explorations south twelve miles and north five miles, the continuance of this strata is reported, and the mineral said to be equally abundant, and from twelve to eighteen feet in thickness: so that without allowing any golden hopes to puzzle my prophetic vision of the future, I would predict for California a Peruvian harvest of the precious metals, as soon as a sufficiency of miners can be obtained."

Brewerton left San Francisco in March and went to Los Angeles, where he awaited Carson, who arrived there during April, and the two finally left on their long journey on the 4th of May.   Besides official dispatches, Carson carried ordinary mail, as Brewerton himself states (p. 114, this text).   This is corroborated by Sherman, who wrote from Monterey on April 10th, "The time is rapidly approaching when Lieutenant Carson . . . will start for home.   He goes from Los Angeles to Santa Fé and thence to St. Louis where he will put his mail in the Post-Office.'' Lieutenant Hollingsworth also noted in his diary under date of April 17th, at Los Angeles, that Carson was preparing to leave. The exact time of arrival of either Brewerton or Carson is not known, but Brewerton reached Independence under ''the meridian heat of an August sun.'' Carson, who went on ahead from Santa Fé, must have reached Fort Leavenworth early in August.

The letter dated April 1st, which appeared in the *Herald* on the 19th of August, must have been in the mail which Carson brought East. As he did not leave for more than a month after the date of the letter, there was ample time for it to have reached Los Angeles. The time of Carson's arrival at Fort Leavenworth would accord with the normal period that the letter would take to reach St. Louis and the Eastern mail, so as to be delivered to the *Herald* and printed on the 19th.

Lieutenant William Tecumseh Sherman, later the General of the March to the Sea, was then Adjutant General under Colonel Mason, the military governor. In his *Memoirs,* he says that the first news he had of the discovery was in the spring of 1848, when two men came to the governor's office as agents of Captain Sutter in an attempt to acquire title to the location of the mill, and that these men brought about a half ounce of gold. Sutter told Sherman afterwards that in February or March James W. Marshall brought down the news from the mill to the fort, some forty miles, with the samples later seen by Sherman. According to Sherman, the Captain did not attach much importance to it, but as a precaution immediately sent the two men to apply for a preëmption of the place. That it must have been the earlier month is shown by the diary and account of Henry W. Bigler, whose contemporary record determined the exact date of the epochal discovery by Marshall in the tail-race of the new sawmill at Coloma. It was on the 24th of January that Bigler recorded the finding of "some kind of mettle that looks like goald." A few days later, he says, provisions ran short, and Marshall went to the fort, with samples of the gold; and about a week later Sutter came to the mill for the first time. The Captain sent his emissaries to Colonel Mason directly after his first report from Marshall. In fact Bigler entered in his diary on February 12th, that Sutter and Marshall had already sent to the government to have the claim secured. Accordingly it must have been in February that Sherman saw the gold from the tail-race, and well before the publication in the *Californian*. So Sherman and Mason learned at an early date of the existence of the placers, even though they may have had no idea of their value or extent.

The first official announcement and confirmation of

the richness of the gold diggings was in the President's Message, December 5th, 1848. To this was attached the report of Colonel Mason, actually written by Lieutenant Sherman. The Message contains the following:

"It was known that mines of the precious metals existed to a considerable extent in California at the time of its acquisition. [The treaty was Feb. 2, 1848.] Recent discoveries render it probable that these mines are more extensive and valuable than was anticipated. The accounts of the abundance of gold in that territory are of such an extraordinary character as would scarcely command belief were they not corroborated by the authentic reports of officers in the public service who have visited the mineral district and derived the facts which they detail from personal observation. Reluctant to credit the reports in general circulation as to the quantity of gold, the officer commanding our forces in California visited the mineral district in July last, for the purpose of obtaining accurate information on the subject. When he visited the country there were about 4,000 persons engaged in collecting gold."

Since the finding of gold at Sutter's Mill was known to Colonel Mason long before Carson left, some mention of it must have been incorporated in the dispatches he bore, and it must have been to these reports that President Polk referred in the opening sentences of the Message as quoted.

Stray items regarding the existence of gold in California had been appearing in Eastern papers for months. The first mention was in the New York *Herald* for August 19th, 1848. In the same paper on the 10th day of October, there were a few lines, part of a communication from Santa Fé, to the effect that B. Chouteau, who left California on the 4th day of July, reported that $2,000 in two pieces of virgin gold had been found near San Francisco. On November 13th came news of gold by way of England, reprinted from the London *Standard* of the 12th day of October, and on the 30th of November, a similar item from the Baltimore *Sun.*

In no other way than by the mail carried by Carson could it have reached the East so soon. As far as is known, Carson was the only courier to cross the continent from California in an easterly direction that year. Joe Meek left the Coast in January, and made a record journey, but he went from Oregon on behalf of the newly organized provisional government. It is also known that several Mormons with a few Gentiles left San Francisco for Salt Lake City and perhaps the Eastern states. Most of them, and it may be all, stopped in Utah, and there is no record of how fast or how far any of them proceeded beyond Salt Lake City. Bigler's diary says that the party planned to leave Sutter's Mill on the 14th of April, after spending a week there. Other Mormon ac-

counts show that they had such difficulties in the
Sierra Nevada with snow and unfamiliar trails that
during one period of twenty-three days the advance
was only forty miles. In addition they were
harassed by Indians who stole many of their horses.
Under such circumstances it is impossible that any
of them could have won through to the Missouri as
soon as the experienced Carson.

The difficulties of communication at the time are
well set forth by Sherman, telling of the problem of
sending the Mason Report to the President, a few
months after Carson's departure. He says: "As
yet we had no regular mail to any part of the United
States, but mails had come to us at long intervals,
around Cape Horn, and one or two overland. I
well remember the first overland mail. It was
brought by Kit Carson in saddlebags from Taos . . .
As soon as we returned from our first visit to the
gold mines, it became important to send home positive knowledge of this valuable discovery. The
means of communication with the United States were
very precarious, and I suggested to Colonel Mason
that a special courier ought to be sent."

Second Lieutenant Loeser was detailed to carry
the report, which was dated August 17, 1848, together with an oyster can full of gold as ocular
proof of the richness of the mines. A vessel was
chartered which took the messenger to Peru, where

he trans-shipped to "the English steamer of October" to Panama, thence to Jamaica, to New Orleans, and to Washington. The report was delivered to the President barely in time to be put in the Message to Congress. In fact, Sherman, as he says in his *Memoirs*, thought it arrived too late for this. So the best that could be done with this report, considered so important, was to have it delivered in Washington in three and a half months; which was almost exactly the same interval as that between the departure of Brewerton and Carson on May 4th and the publication of the *Herald* letter of August 19th. The slowness of communication is further shown by the fact that official news of the signing of the Peace Treaty with Mexico on February 2nd did not reach the authorities in California until September.

Although both Carson and Brewerton must have heard something of the discovery, neither of them could have attached much importance to it. At the time of their departure, there was no excitement anywhere except at the very scene, and they could not then have imagined the outcome. Brewerton says nothing on the subject, nor does Carson; and indeed it is probable that neither of them ever learned that they bore the written tidings. Carson may have carried an oral message, but he was always known as close-mouthed, and was not the man to disclose an official secret either during the performance of his duty or ever afterward, so his silence means nothing.

Carson showed the way to California to Frémont, guided the troops of Kearny to the completion of the conquest and established the routes later followed by the Forty-Niners; so it was entirely fitting that he should have been the man to carry to his government and the people of the East the first word of the gold that was destined the next year to lure a hundred thousand Argonauts to the new Eldorado.

SKETCH OF LIFE OF GEORGE DOUGLAS BREWERTON

George Douglas Brewerton was born in Newport, Rhode Island, on the 3rd day of June, 1827, the eldest son of General Henry and Caroline Louise (Knight) Brewerton. The General had a long and distinguished career in the army. He graduated from West Point at the head of his class, and was commissioned in the Engineer Corps. He was active in the construction of coast defenses and various river and harbor improvements. From 1832 to 1836 he was in charge of the building of the famous Cumberland Road, and from 1845 to 1852 was Superintendent of the Military Academy at West Point. The mother came of an old Rhode Island family, which included Edward Greene Malbone, the well-known artist. To him can be traced the artistic talents of the subject of this sketch.

George Douglas Brewerton spent his youth at or near the Atlantic seaboard, where the father was engaged in engineering work. While living at West Point, he took advantage of the opportunity to study drawing under Professor Robert Walter Weir, the instructor of several generations of cadets whose

sketches of the scenery and natural features of the
West enrich many of the government explorationary
reports.

On the breaking out of the Mexican War, Brewerton sought a place in the army. On August 15th,
1846, at Fort Columbus, Governor's Island, New
York Harbor, he was mustered into service as a
second lieutenant of Captain John E. Brackett's
Company (C), First New York Infantry Volunteers.

General Brewerton had been a protégé of Governor Daniel D. Tompkins, afterwards Vice-President
for two terms under Monroe, while Jonathan D.
Stevenson, who recruited the regiment, had been
private secretary to the Vice-President, and it was
doubtless because of this connection that young
George Douglas selected this particular organiza-
tion.

The regiment, under command of Colonel Stevenson, sailed for California September 26th, 1846, and
Brewerton's ship, the *Loo Choo*, rounded the Horn
and came to anchor in San Francisco Bay exactly
six months later.

Company C took post at Sonoma, where Brewerton remained until November, 1847, when he was
transferred to Company K, stationed at the Presidio,
San Francisco. From the latter company he was
again transferred to the First United States Dra-

goons, commanded by Colonel Richard B. Mason, the military governor of California.

From the volunteer service he was appointed to the regular army, a commission in the First United States Infantry dating from the 22nd day of May, 1847, having been issued to him. He was ordered to cross the plains and join his new regiment at its station in Mississippi. It was to report for duty in accordance with these instructions that he set out on the journey which forms the text of the present narrative. For four years he saw service at various border posts, and after a promotion to the rank of First Lieutenant on the 26th day of June, 1850, resigned from the army on the 31st day of December, 1852, while at Fort Clark, Texas.

For several years after leaving the army, he engaged in newspaper work and writing for the magazines, while he continued to develop his skill as an artist. He was a special correspondent for the New York *Times,* and in 1854 was sent by the New York *Herald* to Kansas Territory to report the Border War there. His experiences were the basis of his book, *The War in Kansas,* published in 1856. During his stay in Kansas, he studied law in the office of Judge Scrugham at Lecompton and was admitted to the bar on the 1st day of May, 1857.

During the Civil War he wrote several manuals of military training, entitled respectively *The Autom-*

aton Regiment, The Automaton Company and *The Automaton Battery.* These were widely used in the instruction of recruits. The command of a New York Volunteer Regiment was offered to him but declined, although later he served on the staff of General Rufus Saxton with the rank of Colonel.

In 1866 and 1867, he was pastor of the Baptist Church of Annsville, but was compelled to give up this ministry on account of ill health.

He wrote two more books, *Fitzpoodle at Newport,* a satirical poem, and *Ada Lewis, the Heroine of Lime Rock,* concerning a light-house keeper's daughter who had made several rescues of shipwrecked sailors. Upon the publication of these books in 1869, he forsook the pen for the brush, except for occasional contributions to the Brooklyn *Eagle,* mostly of verse; and in 1893 he assisted Julian Hawthorne in editing a *History of Washington the Evergreen State.*

Most of his work was on landscapes, and to obtain the effects he desired, he developed a new medium employing a combination of pastels with oil which was highly successful. He maintained a studio in Brooklyn, near Borough Hall, and lived in that city most of the later period of his career, although he made frequent and often prolonged trips, particularly to the far West and South-west, where he found the scenes best suited to his talent and taste.

As the years passed, Colonel Brewerton, as he came to be known, was a familiar figure in the neighborhood of his studio. Tall, slender, of an erect military carriage, and with white hair and beard, he attracted attention wherever he appeared. His manner was courtly and genial, and he made a welcome addition to any gathering, for his descriptions of the incidents of his varied experience, pictured in a retentive memory, held his hearers spellbound. He delighted to lecture to groups of school children on his adventures and on the manners and customs of the Indians he had encountered in the early days.

His long and picturesque life came to an end at Fordham, New York, in his seventy-fourth year, on the 31st day of January, 1901.

A RIDE WITH KIT CARSON

CHAPTER I

FROM LOS ANGELES TO THE MOJAVE

By ship from San Francisco—Arrival at San Pedro—
Journey to Los Angeles—Description of Pueblo de
Los Angeles—Arrival of Carson—Camp at Bridge
Creek—Preparations for journey—The start—The
order of march—The last house—The Cajon Pass.

IT was some time in the boisterous month of March,
1848, that I found myself on board the good ship
Barrington, then lying in the harbor of San Francisco; but only waiting the arrival of passengers to
take her departure for Monterey, Santa Barbara,
and San Pedro; the last-named port being the place,
which I hoped, with the assistance of favoring winds,
shortly to reach. I say I found myself on board
the *Barrington;* now be it understood, that my finding myself in so unstable a position as that of a
ship's deck, was the result of no particular whim
or fancy of mine own, but rather in accordance with
the mandate of an authoritative old gentleman, then
holding military sway in the Californias: which
mandate having come in true official form, duly
signed and sealed by order, I, as an humble lieutenant in the service of "Uncle Sam," felt bound to

31

obey its requirements; with (to quote from the document aforesaid) "as little delay as possible."

San Francisco, in those palmy days of the olden time—at least five years ago—was not even a dim foreshadowing of the present capital of our new "El Dorado," and, consequently, the departure of the only vessel boasting three masts then in the harbor was a kind of epoch, or red-letter day, with the majority of the population. Even the usually deserted beach was enlivened by parties of sauntering Californians, who watched our movements with a sort of idle curiosity, smoking their eternal *cigarritos,* or uttering an occasional *caramba,* as the strong wind sweeping down the bay disturbed the sand and dust, and sent its blinding shower against their faces.

But adieu to these discursive observations. Here come our tardy fellow-voyagers—but three in number, it is true—but far too important personages to be left behind. Our anchor rises rapidly to the bows, the seamen singing gayly to the chorus of "Fare you well, California gals; cheerily, oh, cheerily." And now, the Yerba Buena hills having given back the last echo, we lose our hold upon the oozy bottom, our white wings are fairly spread and fairly filled, and San Francisco, with its sandy streets, and low adobe houses, becomes a mere speck in the distance.

But as it is my purpose to carry the reader with me to a dry and torrid land; and as I have no desire to toss him upon the long surging swells of the Pacific, I will leave it to his imagination to fill up the hiatus of ten days of alternate ship and shore, storms and sunshine, head winds and fair; with all the weary catalogue of indescribable nothings which while away the hours for the traveler over the trackless roads of ocean; suffice it to say, that on the morning of the eleventh day from our departure we anchored safely in the harbor of San Pedro, some five hundred miles down the coast.

The *town* of San Pedro, at the time of which I am writing, consisted of only one *rancho,* or Mexican farm-house, then owned and occupied by an adventurous American, who received us with great hospitality, and very kindly offered my friend Dr. D.[1] and myself, horses to convey us to the Pueblo de los Angeles (City of the Angels), a town some sixteen miles inland; at which place I expected to meet the future companions of my journey, and make the necessary preparations for encountering the perils of a trip through the Great Sahara of North America.

It is difficult for the quiet denizens of a city, whose most memorable experience of life on shipboard is confined to the miseries of a rough night in a steamer

[1] See notes at end of volume.

off Point Judith, to appreciate the almost ecstatic
feelings of delight which stir the heart of a lands-
man, upon being released from the narrow limits of
a ship's deck and cabin. The very earth seems
greener, and the sky brighter; in fact, all nature
seems to be in holiday-trim, and to have ordered a
new suit in honor of his arrival; at least, it so appeared to me when, on the day following our land-
ing, the rising sun saw, or "might have seen" (as
a distinguished modern novelist says), my friend
and myself mounted upon noble horses, and all prepared to take the road for Los Angeles. As usual
in such cases, our host and his family had turned out
in force to make their *adios* and see us off; and,
considering the number of persons, I do not believe
that I ever witnessed a greater scene of noise and
confusion. Every discordant sound, of which a
California farm-yard is so prolific, seemed present,
and doubly magnified to grace the occasion. Don-
keys brayed, Mexicans chattered, cocks crew, every
horse in the *corral,* or horse-yard, seemed determined to give us his farewell neigh; and amid the
almost stunning din I could with difficulty catch the
parting words of our host: "Good-by; never trouble
yourselves about the horses—but take good care of
my saddles." These latter articles, I would remark,
being then, in the almost primitive state of society
existing in California, regarded by their owners as

more valuable than the animals who carried them.

The whole, or nearly the whole of our road to Los Angeles, traversed a rolling prairie, sometimes dotted with groves of stunted trees, but for the most part presenting long slopes and ridges of grassy fields, rich at that season of the year in

STREET IN THE PUEBLO LOS ANGELES.

flowers of every dye; while here and there appeared a *rancho,* where the cattle lying lazily in the shade, and the children playing at their favorite game of lassoing each other, gave animation to the scene, and completed the painting of a beautiful and ever-varying picture. Putting our good steeds to their work, they soon took a long and steady gallop, which brought us rapidly over the ground; and ere many hours had elapsed, the white-walled buildings of Los Angeles opened upon our view.

Leaving my friend at the door of his own domicile, I wended my way to the mess-room of the military gentlemen stationed there, and received from the dragoon and volunteer officers a kind and hospitable welcome. Mr. Christopher Carson (or, as he is better known, Kit Carson), the guide and leader of the party which I was to accompany, not being in town, although soon expected, I was obliged to defer my preparations until I could obtain the aid of his advice and experience; in the meantime I amused myself with visiting every point of interest about the town, riding out, smoking, and now and then flirting with some fair "señorita," thus managing, between pleasant friends and dark eyes, to pass the few days prior to Carson's arrival pleasantly, if not profitably.

The Pueblo de Los Angeles has a population of several hundred souls; and boasts a church, a padre, and three or four American shops; the streets are narrow, and the houses generally not over one story high, built of adobes, the roofs flat and covered with a composition of gravel mixed with a sort of mineral pitch, which the inhabitants say they find upon the sea-shore. This mode of roofing gives a perfectly waterproof covering, but has the rather unpleasant disadvantage of melting in warm weather, and in running down, fringes the sides of the buildings with long *pitchicles* (if we may be allowed to coin a word), thus giving to the houses an exceedingly grotesque appearance; when the heat is extreme, pools of pitch are formed upon the ground. The adobe is a brick, made of clay, and baked in the sun. Walls built of this matcrial, from the great thickness necessary to secure strength, are warmer in winter, and cooler in summer, and are therefore better adapted to the climate than either wood or ordinary brick. In most respects, the town differs but little from other Mexican villages.

Just as I was beginning to weary of the comparatively idle life which we were leading, a friend informed me that Carson had arrived, and would shortly join our party at the mess-room. The name of this celebrated mountaineer had become in the ears of Americans residing in California a familiar household word; and I had frequently listened to wild tales of daring feats which he had performed. The narrators being oftentimes men noted for their immense powers of endurance, I had caught, almost insensibly, a portion of their enthusiasm, and loved to dwell upon the theme. It is scarcely wonderful, then, that I should in my mind's eye (a quiet little studio of mine own, where I conjure up all sorts of fancies) not only sketch, but, by degrees, fill up the details of a character which I thought must resemble the guide and companion of the adventurous Frémont. My astonishment therefore may better be conceived than described when I turn both sides of the canvas to the reader, by drawing the picture as I had dreamed it out, and then endeavoring to portray the man as he really is.

The Kit Carson of my *imagination* was over six feet high—a sort of modern Hercules in his build —with an enormous beard, and a voice like a roused lion, whose talk was all of—

"Stirring incidents by flood and field."

The *real* Kit Carson I found to be a plain, simple, unostentatious man; rather below the medium height, with brown, curling hair, little or no beard, and a voice as soft and gentle as a woman's. In fact, the hero of a hundred desperate encounters, whose life had been mostly spent amid wildernesses, where the white man is almost unknown, was one of Dame Nature's gentlemen—a sort of article which she gets up occasionally, but nowhere in better style than among the backwoods of America.

I will not attempt to sketch Kit's earlier life and adventures; Frémont has drawn him with a master's hand, and my inexperienced pen may not improve upon his description.

In making the foregoing remarks, I have only offered my humble testimonial to the sterling worth of a man who, I am proud to say, was my guide, companion, and friend, through some of the wildest regions ever traversed by the foot of man.

"Kit," as I shall often call him, informed me that he had made camp at Bridge Creek, some fifteen miles distant from the Pueblo, on our road to the Great Pass, by which we purposed crossing the California mountains and entering into the solitudes of the Sandy Desert. This camp at Bridge Creek had been established by Carson with the view of preparing our animals (many of whom had seen hard service) for the long and tedious journey before them; and a better locality for our purpose could scarcely have been selected. Bridge Creek is a pretty little stream of clear, sweet water, fringed with trees, which afforded plenty of timber for our *corral.* On the plains, in its vicinity, the wild oats grew in luxuriant abundance, furnishing a rich pasturage. As Kit purposed taking up his residence in camp, a variety of reasons induced me to accompany him. For one thing, I had grown heartily tired of fleas, with which the houses in town are densely populated; and, in the second place, I wished to get an insight into the sort of gipsy-life which I must necessarily lead for some months to come. So, having concluded that an immediate commencement of my education in this respect would render its privations easier when the time of trial came, I provided myself with a tin-plate, a tin-cup, which might hold about a quart, for no true mountaineer ever drinks less than that amount of coffee at a sitting

—if he can get it. To these articles I added a common fork, a large bowie-knife, and a rifle;—and thus, having furnished my table and armory, I turned my attention to the bed-chamber portion of the establishment. Here my preparations were equally simple and unpretending: two Mexican blankets serving me at once for mattress, sheets, and pillow-cases, while my saddle gave a rude, but never-failing pillow. Imagine me, then, fully equipped, and prepared to take up my abode under the first tree, if the good of the service should require it.

Late in the afternoon Carson and myself, mounted upon a couple of stout mules, left the Pueblo behind us, and after three hours' riding, over hills and dales so rich in flowers that it seemed as if nature had contemplated the manufacture of a patch-work quilt upon a grand scale, we reached the spot which was to be our abiding place for nearly a month. Here I found the men, twenty in number, who had been hired for the expedition, all busily employed in taking care of our large *caballada* of mules and horses; many of these men were noted woodsmen, old companions of Carson's in his explorations with Frémont; while others, again, were almost as ignorant of mountain life as myself; knowing nothing of the mysteries of a pack-saddle, and keeping at a most respectful distance from the heels of a kicking mule.

Our daily routine of life while sojourning at Bridge Creek was certainly primitive in its simplicity. Shortly after sunrise the camp was awakened, the animals released from their confinement in the *corral,* and driven to water, from thence they were conveyed to the fields of wild oats where each mule being secured by a long *réata* (a kind of strong Mexican rope made by twisting thongs of hide together), to an iron picket-pin driven into the ground, was permitted to graze until sunset, when the drove were again watered and secured in the *corral* for the night. The habits of the Californian mule are rather peculiar. Though very cautious animals when relying solely upon their own judgment—under which circumstances they generally get along very well— they would appear to have a consciousness of their own inferiority, which induces them to entertain a great regard for the sagacity of the horse, and particularly for that of a white mare. Now why the "gray mare" should be the "better horse" in their estimation, I can not say, but such is certainly the fact; and the wily Californians, taking advantage of this amiable weakness, are in the habit of employing a steady old white mare of known gentleness and good character to act as a kind of mother and guide to each drove of unruly mules. This animal is sometimes called the "bell mare" from a large bell which they attach to her neck, to the tinklings of which, sooner or later, every mule in the *caballada* becomes an obedient slave. In conformity with so excellent a custom we had destined for this service an old gray mare belonging to one of our party; and I often amused an idle hour by watching the court paid her by the mulish crowd. To be allowed to graze in her immediate vicinity was evidently considered a privilege by every long-eared lady and gentleman in the herd; and to obtain this much coveted position many was the quarrel, and many the spiteful bite and kick given and received. But the old mare, like a philosophical beast as she was, looked upon all their attentions with great scorn and indifference; or only noticed them, when annoyed by the tumult around her, by using both teeth and heels with wonderful dexterity, and showering her blows with great impartiality among her four-legged admirers.

For ourselves, we fished, hunted, and practiced rifle-shooting (in which latter accomplishment many of the mountaineers are almost incredibly expert); and when the evening had fairly set in, and the round bright moon peeped slyly down through the trees, we gathered round our fire in the open air, with the blue heavens and broad spreading branches for our canopy, and with these, with songs and stories not the less interesting for being real, and in many cases the personal adventures of their narrators, we whiled away the hours so pleasantly that

LIFE AT BRIDGE CREEK

it was often midnight before we spread our blankets, and laid down to sleep more soundly, and dream more sweetly, than many a man who reclines upon a couch of down.

It was finally determined that we should take the road upon the 4th of May; and having procured four stout mules, already experienced in mountain travel, from the Quartermaster at "Los Angeles" (two for riding, and the same number to pack my baggage and provisions), I purchased, after much bargaining, and many serious misgivings that I had been sorely cheated, two additional mules and one horse; which latter proved to be an animal of terrible experiences, being troubled with some painful internal complaint, which induced him to lie down whenever his rider particularly wished him to stand up. I finally thought that he found the hydropathic treatment beneficial, as he seldom crossed a stream without rolling himself and rider in the water. Having thus got together seven animals I concluded that so far as horse-flesh was concerned I should do well enough; but where to procure a proper servant, or *arriero* as they are called in Mexico, to pack my mules, and take charge of the cooking, was a problem which seemed more than difficult to solve; at last, just as I was beginning to despair, fortune appeared to favor me, and a Mexican presented himself as a candidate for the office of cook, muleteer, and a man of all work. A single glance at Señor Jesús Garcia (I will give only two of his half a dozen names) convinced me that whatever other qualifications he might exhibit he was certainly old, ugly, and possessed of a most villainous cast of countenance. But as it was a sort of last chance with me I was fain to receive him graciously, and after asking a few questions to which Señor Jesús replied with all the volubility for which the Mexicans are famous, I felt fully satisfied that—if one were to believe his own account of his manifold perfections, both as a man and as a muleteer—there had never existed such a paragon of virtue and skill. He could pack a mule in the twinkling of an eye, lasso and ride the wildest horse that ever ran, and as for honesty "El Teniente might load him with bags of uncounted doubloons and he would not steal a single medio."

On the second of May we broke up our camp on the Creek, and returned to Los Angeles, from which point we purposed starting on the morning of the fourth. In the interval we employed ourselves in making our final preparations; drawing rations and ammunition for our men, and dividing our provisions into bags of equal size and weight for the greater convenience of packing. The stores provided for our own mess (which had been increased to four in number by the addition of an old mountain man, a friend of Carson's, and a citizen returning to the States) consisted of pork, coffee, brown sugar, *Penole* and *Atole.*

The two articles last named are peculiarly Mexican, and worthy of a description. Atole is a kind of meal which when prepared forms a very nutritious dish not unlike "mush," both in taste and appearance. Penole is made by parching Indian corn; then grinding it, and mixing with cinnamon and sugar. This condiment is almost invaluable to the travelers in the wildernesses of the Far West; as it requires no fire to cook it, being prepared at a moment's warning by simply mixing it with cold water. It has the further advantage of occupying but little space in proportion to its weight; but when prepared for use, it swells so as nearly to double in quantity. A very small portion is therefore sufficient to satisfy the cravings of hunger. In addition to these matters, we carried with us for our private consumption a small quantity of dried meat; this is also obtained from the Mexicans, who cut the beef into long strips, and then hang it upon a line, exposing it to the influence of the sun and wind until it is thoroughly hardened. When they wish to employ a more rapid process, a rude framework is erected, and on this the strings of meat are laid, a slow fire being kept up underneath until the whole becomes smoked and dried. Beef prepared in this way will keep for a long time, and is generally sold by the Mexican *vara,* or yard.

The morning of the fourth of May at length dawned upon us; and although we were all up with the sun, nine o'clock found our camp in a state of terrible confusion. I have already stated that some of our party were inexperienced hands; and as packing a mule is not always a thing to be learned by intuition, they certainly made an awkward commencement at their new business. I have since thought that it might have been amusing to an uninterested spectator to watch the quiet look of contempt with which our old stagers regarded some poor greenhorn who succeeded in getting the pack upon his mule's back, only to behold it kicked off by the indignant animal, who after performing this feat would turn round to the discomfited packer with a look that seemed to say, ''Well, you haven't traveled, that's certain.''

While others were thus annoyed, I was by no means exempt from my share of vexation; my pattern of a muleteer, Jesús, was nowhere to be found. That paragon of virtue had allowed himself to be seduced by a new pair of boots, and a trifle of clothing which he found in my carpet bag; and if he had not ''sloped to Texas'' he had at all events migrated to parts unknown; and there was I, at the last moment, with seven animals to be taken care of, packed, saddled, or driven, and not a soul to attend to them. Just as I was about giving up in good earnest, a young Mexican came up to me and requested that he might be allowed to fill the vacancy. Upon questioning him Kit recognized him at once. "A greater rascal," said Carson, "I don't think ever lived than that same young Mexican, but he knows how to take care of a mule."

It seems that Juan, such being the name of my new applicant, had crossed the desert once before as a muleteer to an American trader; and to revenge himself for some ill treatment, real or fancied, he had cut holes in the provision bags; by which means their contents were lost upon the road, and both master and man reduced to the very verge of starvation before reaching the settlements. As I could do no better, I concluded to employ him, at the same time making a mental determination to keep a sharp eye upon Master Juan, and bring him up, nautically speaking, with "a round turn" upon the first occasion of transgression.

Juan being thus duly installed as my muleteer in chief, and cook in general, commenced operations *instanter,* by packing my mules with a celerity which fairly astonished me; for in a few moments the heavy loads were properly arranged, and my mule and his own were fairly saddled and bridled. It was fully ten o'clock before our party finally got off. We numbered twenty hired men, three citizens, and three Mexican servants, besides Carson and myself, all well mounted and armed for the most part with "Whitney's rifle," a weapon which I can not too strongly recommend for every description of frontier service, from its great accuracy and little liability to get out of order—an important point in a country where no gunsmith can be found.

The order of our march, unless altered by circumstances, or some peculiar feature of the ground, was as follows. Kit and myself, with one or more of our party, came first, then followed the pack mules and loose animals, and in their rear the remainder of our men, who urged the mules forward by loud cries, and an occasional blow from the ends of their lariats. Our saddles were of the true Mexican pattern, wooden trees covered with leathers called *macheers*. This saddle for service I found far superior to those of American make, being both easier and safer, the great depth of the seat rendering it almost impossible for the animal to dislodge his rider, a fact which partly accounts for the fearless horsemanship for which Mexicans are so famous. Our bridles, formed of twisted hide or horse hair, were ornamented with pieces of copper, and furnished with strong Spanish bits. As for our spurs, they were sharp and heavy enough to have driven an elephant, not to speak of a Californian mule, which I take to be the more unmanageable beast of the two. To finish the details of our equipments, I will describe my own costume as a fair sample of the style of dress which we wore. I was attired in a check or "hickory" shirt as they are called, a pair of buckskin pants, a fringed hunting shirt of the same material, gayly lined with red flannel and ornamented with brass buttons (which last I afterward found useful in trading with the Indians). As for my head gear, my hat would scarcely have passed muster among the "Genins" and "Learys" in Broadway—being nothing more than a broad-brimmed straw of very ordinary texture. To go to the other extremity, my feet were cased in a pair of strong cowhide boots, which reached almost to the knee. My weapons I have already noticed; but among my list of sundries I must not forget my water flask, which was a curiosity in its way, and as I have not as yet taken out a patent for the invention, it may give some ingenious Yankee a new idea. It was a bottle made of porous leather which held half a gallon, and suffered just so much of the liquid to soak through as was requisite to keep the outside constantly wet, so that whenever I desired cool water I had only to hang up my flask, or expose it to a free current of air.

As the first day's march was intended as a sort of trial trip, we determined to make the distance a short one, and encamp for the night at our old stand, Bridge Creek, which, as I have before stated, was directly on our way to the Pass; and it was well that we did so; for though our camping ground was but fifteen miles distant from the Pueblo, our march seemed more like a chapter of accidents than a progressive movement. Many of the mules, saddled for the first time in months, got up all sorts of ungainly antics; and were as vicious and obstinate as possible. We had scarcely cleared the town when a tremendous clatter in our rear apprised me that something was coming; and ere I could turn my head, a pack-mule passed me at the top of her speed, with her head stretched out and her heels flying in the air, while at every jump, the beast flung some article of my personal property, right and left, here a frying-pan, and there a bag of sugar, while Juan came thundering in her wake, swearing indifferently in Spanish and English, and threatening all sorts of personal violence to the long-eared offender. And so we jogged along until sunset. I do not believe that a more tired man, or one more keenly sensible of the luxuries of rest and a good cup of coffee, could have been found that night than myself.

By sunrise the next morning we were on our way to the Pass, and a hard and hot day's ride we had of it. During the day we passed the last house which we were to see until our arrival in the Territory of New Mexico, and I must confess that I turned in my saddle and cast many "a longing, lingering look" behind. Our camp that night was upon a rough and stony hillside within the Pass. I remember well that I felt something more substantial than a crumpled rose-leaf under me during the night; to say nothing of awakening in the morning with an accurate impression of divers small geological specimens in my back and sides. But these were minor difficulties and a mere foretaste of the troubles to come.

CHAPTER II

FROM THE MOJAVE TO THE ARCHILETTE

On the desert—A recalcitrant mule—On the Old Spanish
Trail—The Mexican caravan—A drink à la Byron—
Discipline for Juan—A rattlesnake for bedfellow—
Passage over the desert—Carson's watchfulness—Jor-
nado del Muerto—Bill Williams' horse-stealing expe-
dition—Lost on the desert—Saved by the mule—
Meeting with Indians—Meeting with Joseph Walker—
The pipe of peace—Habits of Digger Indians—A sneak
thief—Signal smoke—The hostage.

AND now, dear reader, as I am about entering
upon the theatre of our more exciting travel, I will
remark that it is not my intention to treat the subject geographically, geologically, or botanically. I
have had a horror of the "ologies" ever since my
days of schoolboy experience, and as Frémont has
described the country, its general features and productions, it would be not only unnecessary, but pre-
sumptuous in me to portray it : I shall therefore con-
fine myself to such scenes of incident and adventure as might prove most interesting; and—thanks
to Indians, hard travel and harder fare—I think
there will be no lack of incident.

My sensations upon viewing the Great Desert for

the first time were certainly peculiar, and I think
that they who know the country will acquit me of
any unmanly feeling, when I say, that, as my eye
wandered over the vast expanse of hot sand and
broken rock, I thought that I should not altogether
dislike "backing out." But we were "in for it,"
and there was no use moralizing. Besides I soon
had matters of more moment to occupy me.

Among my seven animals (of whom, to criticise
them as a body, I can safely say that they appeared
to be about equally made of viciousness, obstinacy,
and a strong disposition to laziness) I found a little
gray mule which I had reserved for my especial
riding. She had her unpleasant peculiarities too,
one of which was that it generally required about
two men to saddle her, one to throw her down, and
one to put the saddle on. Another amiable failing
was a trick which on this occasion I learned to my
cost; though perfectly gentle with her rider fairly
seated, she took advantage of your getting off, to
look quietly round, get your exact position and attitude, then let both heels fly, knock you down, and
be off like the wind. We had just got to the foot
of a long, steep sand hill, when by some ill fortune
I found myself half a mile in the rear of our men,
who were crossing the summit of the ridge; my saddle slipping at the same time, I dismounted to tighten
the girths, when my "gallant gray" at once prac-

APPROACH TO THE GREAT SANDY DESERT.

ticed her favorite manœuvre, leaving me *hors de combat,* doubled up on a heap of sand in company with about fifty pounds of light luggage, in the way of blankets, gun, and ammunition, from which recumbent position I elevated myself just in time to behold my treacherous mule under full sail for the rest of the caballada. Talk about Job's troubles, if you will; it *was* enough to make a minister forget himself. I did swear a little, and once I leveled my rifle at the flying steed; but prudence stepped in and whispered that one live mule was worth ten dead ones—particularly on the road—so I determined to pocket my anger for the present, and shouldering my gun, with a blanket on either arm, I trudged up hill through the deep sands for nearly a mile, when just as I had made up my mind to stop where I was until the Diggers should be pleased to come and take me, Juan galloped up with the truant mule which he had captured with his lasso. I can assure the reader that I was not the only sufferer by the transaction.

Our route for several days lay over a dreary waste, where the eye met the same eternal rock and sand. In fact, the whole country looks more like the crater of an immense volcano than anything else that I can compare it to; or, to use the words of one of our men, he believed "the darned place had been a-fire, and hadn't got quite cool yet." Our general

SAND ROCKS IN THE DESERT

course was by the great Spanish trail, and we made as rapid traveling as possible, with the view of overtaking the large Mexican caravan which was slowly wending its way back to the capital of New Mexico. This caravan consisted of some two or three hundred Mexican traders who go once a year to the Californian coast with a supply of blankets and other articles of New Mexican manufacture; and having disposed of their goods, invest the proceeds in Californian mules and horses, which they drive back across the desert. These people often realize large profits, as the animals purchased for a mere trifle on the coast, bring high prices in Santa Fé. This caravan had left Pueblo de Los Angeles some time before us, and were consequently several days in advance of our party upon the trail—a circumstance which did us great injury, as their large caballada (containing nearly a thousand head) ate up or destroyed the grass and consumed the water at the few camping grounds upon the route.

We finally overtook and passed this party, after some eight days' travel in the Desert. Their appearance was grotesque in the extreme. Imagine upward of two hundred Mexicans dressed in every variety of costume, from the embroidered jacket of the wealthy Californian, with its silver bell-shaped buttons, to the scanty habiliments of the skin-clad Indian, and you may form some faint idea of their

dress.   Their caballada contained not only horses
and mules, but here and there a stray *burro* (Mexican jackass) destined to pack wood across the rugged
hills of New Mexico.   The line of march of this
strange cavalcade occupied an extent of more than

NEW-MEXICAN TRADER.

a mile; and I could not help thinking while observing
their arms and equipments, that a few resolute men
might have captured their property, and driven the
traders like a flock of sheep.   Many of these people
had no fire-arms, being only provided with the
short bow and arrows usually carried by New Mexican herdsmen.   Others were armed with old English muskets, condemned long ago as unserviceable,
which had, in all probability, been loaded for years,
and now bid fair to do more damage at the stock

than at the muzzle. Another description of weapon appeared to be highly prized among them—these were old, worn-out dragoon sabres, dull and rusty, at best a most useless arm in contending with an enemy who fights only from inaccessible rocks and precipices; but when carried under the leathers of the saddle, and tied with all the manifold straps and knots with which the Mexican secures them, perfectly worthless even at close quarters.

Near this motley crowd we sojourned for one night; and passing through their camp after dark, I was struck with its picturesque appearance. Their pack-saddles and bales had been taken off and carefully piled, so as not only to protect them from damp, but to form a sort of barricade or fort for their owner. From one side to the other of these little corrals of goods a Mexican blanket was stretched, under which the trader lay smoking his cigarrito, while his Mexican servant or slave—for they are little better—prepared his coffee and "atole."

Not long after leaving the great caravan I had gone aside from our trail, and found a small quantity of water, which looked clear and tempting, in a deep crevice among the rocks. The noon-day sun shone fiercely upon the burning sand, and my mouth was parched with thirst; but though longing to drink, the water was in so inaccessible a position that, without some vessel in which to draw it from the chasm, my case would have been but little better than that of Tantalus. I looked in vain for my ordinary drinking cup, but Señor Juan, with great forethought for his own comfort, had fastened it to his saddle before starting. As I stood racking my brain to discover some expedient which might overcome the difficulty, I espied a human skeleton near me. A thought struck me. I remembered Byron, and his libations from the skull; and, revolting as it would have been under different circumstances, my strong necessity compelled me to make use of it. So I drank a most grateful draught of water from the bleaching bone, and then sat down to moralize upon the event, and wonder to whom it had belonged, and how its owner died; the result of all of which was, that I felt much obliged to the unknown individual for the use of that which could by no possibility be of any further service to him; and as a committee of one, sitting alone in the desert by the side of the fountain, I voted him my thanks accordingly.

I have heretofore briefly mentioned my Mexican servant Juan, to whom Carson had given so indifferent a character. This scapegrace had for some days shown a disposition to give trouble in various ways; but we had come to no open rupture until one afternoon, when riding in the advance, I looked back and observed the *réata* of my pack-mule dragging upon the ground. Calling to Juan to secure it, I rode on, thinking that my orders had been attended to. Now it so happened at that particular moment that Señor Juan was engaged with the assistance of a Mexican friend and his cigarrito in making himself exceedingly comfortable; and upon again turning my head I found my *réata* in a worse way than before. "Now," said Kit, "that fellow is trying which is to be the master, you or he, and I should advise you to give him a lesson which he will remember: if we were nearer the settlements I would not recommend it, for he would certainly desert and carry your animals with him; but as it is, he will not dare to leave the party, for fear of the Indians." As I fully concurred in Carson's opinion, and felt moreover that the period had arrived for bringing up Señor Juan with the "round turn" I had mentally promised him, I simply rode back, and without any particular explanation, knocked the fellow off his mule. It was the first lesson and the last which I found it necessary to read him. Juan gave me, it is true, a most diabolical look upon remounting, which made me careful of my pistols for a night or two afterward; but he was conquered, and in future I had no reason to complain of any negligence.

The only living creatures which inhabit the desert,

except the prowling Diggers, are a small rabbit which burrows in the ground, existing I can scarce say how, lizards in great quantities, and a small but very venomous description of rattlesnake; with the last named reptile I was destined during my sojourn in this region to have anything but an agreeable interview.

It was a bright moonlight night; I had, as was my custom, spread my saddle leathers for a bed, and drawn by blanket loosely around me. Weary with the day's march I had been sleeping soundly for several hours, when about midnight I awoke suddenly, with an unaccountable feeling of dread: it must have been a sort of instinct which prompted me, for in a moment I was upon my feet, and then upon removing my blanket found a rattlesnake swollen with rage and poison, coiled and ready to strike. I drew away the *macheers* which served as a mattress, intending to kill the reptile, when to my astonishment it glided away, making its escape into a small opening in the ground directly beneath my bed. The whole matter was explained at once; I had retired early, and in arranging my couch had spread it directly near the door of his snakeship's domicile. The snake had probably been out to see a neighbor, and getting home after I was asleep, felt a gentlemanly unwillingness to disturb me, and as I had taken possession of his dwelling he took

part of my sleeping place, crawling under the blanket
where he must have lain quietly by my side, until
I rolled over and disturbed him. I can scarcely
say that I slept much more that night, and even
Carson admitted that it made him a little nervous.
Had I been bitten our only remedy would have been
some common whisky, which we carried with us in
case of such an accident. It is a fact worth knowing,
that in the mountains strong liquor is considered a
certain preventive to any ill effects from snake-bites;
to administer it properly it must be given at once,
and in large quantities, until the patient is fully
under its influence.

Our daily routine of life in the desert had a sort
of terrible sameness about it; we rode from fifteen
to fifty miles a day, according to the distance from
water; occasionally after a long drive halting for
twenty-four hours, if the scanty grass near the camping grounds would permit it, to rest and recruit our
weary cattle; among our men there was but little
talking and less laughing and joking, even by the
camp-fire, while traversing these dreary wastes; the
gloomy land by which we were surrounded, scanty
food, hard travel, and the consciousness of continual
peril, all tended to restrain the exhibition of animal
spirits. Carson, while traveling, scarcely spoke; his
keen eye was continually examining the country, and
his whole manner was that of a man deeply im-

pressed with a sense of responsibility. We ate but twice a day, and then our food was so coarse and scanty, that it was not a pleasure, but a necessity. At night every care was taken to prevent surprise; the men took turns in guarding the animals, while our own mess formed the camp guard of the party. In an Indian country it is worthy of remembrance that a mule is by far the best sentry; they discover either by their keen sense of smell, or of vision, the vicinity of the lurking savage long before the mountaineer, experienced as he is, can perceive him. If thus alarmed, the mule shows its uneasiness by snorting and extending the head and ears toward the object of distrust.

During this journey I often watched with great curiosity Carson's preparations for the night. A braver man than Kit perhaps never lived, in fact I doubt if he ever knew what fear was, but with all this he exercised great caution. While arranging his bed, his saddle, which he always used as a pillow, was disposed in such a manner as to form a barricade for his head; his pistols half cocked were laid above it, and his trusty rifle reposed beneath the blanket by his side, where it was not only ready for instant use, but perfectly protected from the damp. Except now and then to light his pipe, you never caught Kit exposing himself to full glare of the camp fire. He knew too well the treacherous character of the tribes among whom we were traveling; he had seen men killed at night by an unseen foe, who, veiled in darkness, stood in perfect security while he marked and shot down the mountaineer clearly seen by the fire-light. "No, no, boys," Kit would say, "hang round the fire if you will, it may do for you if you like it, but I don't want to have a Digger slip an arrow into me, when I can't see him."

A rather amusing story is told of Kit's quickness of action in time of danger. Some inexperienced mountaineer had given the alarm of Indians during his tour of guard duty at night, or as Western men sometimes express it "stampeded the camp"; Kit sprang to his feet in an instant and while yet half asleep, seeing some dark object advancing upon him through the long grass, seized one of his unerring pistols and shot, not an Indian, but his own particular riding mule right through the head.

When the hour for our departure from camp had nearly arrived, Kit would rise from his blanket and cry "Catch up"; two words which in mountain parlance mean "Prepare to start"; and these words once uttered, the sooner a man got ready the better; in a moment the whole scene would be changed, the men who just before were lounging about the fires, or taking a journey to the land of dreams, were now upon their feet, and actively employed in bringing

INDIANS CASTING STONES DOWN UPON THE TRAVELERS.

up refractory mules, who, true to their obstinate nature, and finding that their services were about to be required, declining any forward movement, except upon compulsion. This generally called forth a volley of oaths from their enraged drivers—English, Spanish and Canadian French being all prolific in objurgations; until at length the loads were fairly secured, saddles put on, and the pack-mules having been gathered together were started upon the trail; the old bell-mare leading off with a gravity quite equal to the responsibility of her office. Kit waited for nobody; and woe to the unfortunate tyro in mountain travel who discovered to his sorrow that packs would work, bags fall off, and mules show an utter disregard for the preservation of one's personal property. A man thus circumstanced soon learns to pack a mule as it should be done, at first, put on his saddle as it ought to be put on, and keep his arms in serviceable order; or if he don't, Heaven help him; the sooner he gets back to the settlements the better.

In crossing the Desert it is often necessary to march long distances without water; these dry stretches are called by the Mexicans "jornadas"; the literal meaning of the word being a journey, but in instances like the present it refers to the absence of water upon the route traveled. On the "jornada" of which I am about to speak, which is sometimes called the "Jornada del Muerto" (the journey of death),[2] the distance from one water hole to another can not be less than eighty miles; and on account of the animals it is highly important that it should be traveled at once; to accomplish this we started about three o'clock in the afternoon and reached the other side of the jornada late in the morning of the following day, the greater part of the distance being gone over by moonlight. I shall never forget the impression which that night's journey left upon my mind. Sometimes the trail led us over large basins of deep sand, where the trampling of the mules' feet gave forth no sound; this added to the almost terrible silence, which ever reigns in the solitudes of the desert, rendered our transit more like the passage of some airy spectacle where the actors were shadows instead of men. Nor is this comparison a constrained one, for our way-worn voyagers with their tangled locks and unshorn beards (rendered white as snow by the fine sand with which the air in these regions is often filled) had a weird and ghost-like look, which the gloomy scene around, with its frowning rocks and moonlit sands, tended to enhance and heighten.

There were other matters, too, to render the view impressive: scattered along our route we found numerous skeletons of horses, who at some former period had dropped down and died by the wayside.

The frequent recurrence of these bleaching bones in a road so lonely, induced me to ask some explanation in regard to them of an old trapper belonging to our party. He informed me, that many years before, Billy Williams, a mountaineer almost as distinguished as Carson himself, had, in some interval of catching beaver and killing Indians, found time to gather a band of mountain men, with the view of undertaking a sort of piratical expedition to the coast of Lower California. In this enterprise he succeeded so far as to enter California, help himself to upward of fifteen hundred head of mules and horses, and regain the desert without losing a man. But from this point his troubles began. The Californians, disapproving of this summary mode of treating their property, determined to pursue and retake it by force; and to carry out their design, followed closely upon the trail of Williams's party, with nearly two hundred men. Finding himself pursued, the mountaineer, whose men were not over thirty in number, pushed on with all possible speed; and in crossing the great jornada, lost from fatigue and overdriving nearly one thousand head of his ill-gotten booty. Rendered desperate, he encamped at a water-hole, some fifteen miles distant from the termination of the jornada, at which latter point his pursuers had already arrived; Williams remarking to his men, "Well, boys, we have lost the most of our caballada, but we have five hundred animals left; and as we must recruit our stock, we will just stop where we are till we have done so; and, in the meantime, if those Mexicans want to get their animals, let them come and take them, if they can.'' In accordance with this determination Billy's people waited three days; but so far as the coming of their enemies was concerned, waited in vain; their courage had evidently failed them; and, although they could pursue a retreating foe, they felt no inclination to face the rifles of American hunters, who had turned like a stag at bay. At length, growing tired of inaction, and exasperated by the loss which he had already sustained, Williams proposed to his comrades to visit the Californian camp by night, and steal the horses upon which their pursuers had followed them. To this they assented; and that evening took from their enemies every horse and mule which they had with them, leaving them to return as they best might. This feat having been thus successfully performed, the Americans went on their way rejoicing. But alas for human expectations! as though to mete out a sort of even-handed justice, it was destined that they should be attacked by the Indians, who drove off their whole caballada, leaving them to find their way back to Santa Fé on foot. I will add that it is rumored that Williams curses the Indians heartily whenever he tells the tale.

Such is the story; but beyond the dry bones upon the jornada, I can bear no witness to its truth.

I was not permitted to pass this portion of the desert without meeting with an adventure, which even now makes my heart beat quicker when I think of it.

When almost midway in the jornada, we entered upon what appeared, by the uncertain light, to be an immense circular basin of sand, surrounded by a range of mountains so distant that the eye could barely make out their dim outlines against the moonlit sky. This sand plain must have been fully eighteen miles in diameter; and we had barely got into it when one of my pack-mules kicked off her load; and by so doing, rendered it necessary for Juan and myself to dismount, collect the bags, and repack the animal; an operation which, as the mule was extremely restive, occupied some time to perform. When we were ready to start, I directed Juan to go ahead with the pack-mule, while I followed slowly in his rear. Now, among other imperfections, it is my misfortune to be very absent-minded; and having fallen into some train of thought which I wished to ravel out, I threw the reins upon the neck of my mule, and jogged along slowly, until a sudden stumble warned me that we were getting into rocky ground again; and upon looking round to discover the whereabouts of our

party, I found that they were not only out of sight,
but out of hearing. Now as this had happened to
me before, I did not give myself any particular uneasiness; but alighted, thinking that I could easily
retrace my road by the track of the mules' hoofs
in the sand, and thus return until I struck the back
trail of our caballada, when it would be an easy
matter to rejoin them; but my horror can scarcely
be conceived, when I discovered that the strong
wind which was blowing had filled the hoof tracks
almost as fast as they had been made, so that all
trace of my route was gone. My situation was certainly one to appall the stoutest heart; in the depths
of an almost trackless wilderness, five hundred miles
from the nearest settlements, and perfectly ignorant
as I was, not only of the locality of the water hole,
but even of the general course which Kit intended
taking, I saw no prospect before me but a lingering
death from starvation, with none to witness my
sufferings—or, at best, to be murdered by the
Indians, who were continually lurking about the
Spanish trail. My very mule seemed to sympathize
with my uneasiness, by snorting wildly, tossing her
head in the air, and beating the ground with her
hoofs. At length, a hope dawned upon me. I had
often heard of the great sagacity of the Mexican
mules, and the astonishing distances at which they
will scent water; and I felt that if I was to be saved,

the mule's instinct must be my preservation. So springing upon her back, I gave her the spur, at the same time uttering the cry used by Mexican muleteers to encourage their animals; then flinging the reins loosely upon her back, I left her to take whatever course she pleased. For a moment, the animal faltered and seemed uncertain, then bounded madly forward, snuffed the air, and put her head to the ground. A moment more, and with a wild cry and a shake of the head, she was off at a rapid gallop, never halting, save now and then to snuff the sand, until she had carried me safely into the very midst of our party. I need scarcely say that I felt very much like a man who had been badly scared, and had only just begun to get over it. I remember, too, making a resolution never to be left behind again —which I kept, at least, a week.

The Pau-Eutaw or Digger Indians (so called from the roots which they dig from the ground and on which they depend for the greater portion of their miserable subsistence) first made their appearance shortly after we had crossed the great jornada. Our camp was then situated upon the borders of a little stream, where a few scanty patches of grass afforded some refreshment to our tired beasts; and our party, with few exceptions, besides the watchful horse-guard, were stretched upon the ground resting wearily after the long night's ride, which we had just accomplished. Carson, who was lying beside me, suddenly raised himself upon his elbow, and turning to me, asked: "Do you see those Indians?" at the same time pointing to the crest of one of the gravelly, bluff-like hills with which we were surrounded. After a careful examination of the locality, I was obliged to reply in the negative. "Well," said Kit, "I saw an Indian's head there just now, and there are a party of at least a dozen more, or I am much mistaken." Scarcely were the words out of his mouth when a savage rose to his full height, as if he had grown from the rocks which fringed the hill top: this fellow commenced yelling in a strange guttural tongue, at the same time gesticulating violently with his hands; this he intended as a declaration of friendship; and Kit rising up, answered him in his own language, "Tigabu, tigabu" (friend, friend). After a little delay, and an evident consultation with his people, the old Digger (for such he proved to be) came, at first rapidly and then more slowly, toward us, descending the steep hillside with an agility astonishing in so aged a being. Carson advanced a short distance to meet him, and again renewed his assurance of our friendship; but it was not until the old man had been presented with some trifling gift that he seemed fully at his ease, and yelled to his companions to join him. This they did with evident caution, coming into our camp two or three at a time until they numbered upward of a dozen. The old man had evidently been sent as a sort of a forlorn hope, to fall a victim, should we be inclined to hostility. Our Indian visitors soon gave us to understand that they were hungry; to meet this demand upon our hospitality we ordered more coffee put upon the fire, and presented them with what little remained of our dried beef, which having got wet was now both spoiled and mouldy. This, disgusting as it was, they ate voraciously; but in regard to the coffee, they seemed somewhat doubtful, until we had ourselves drank of it, when they followed our example without further hesitation, and soon emptied the kettle. In fact, had we been disposed to furnish the material, they would have devoured our whole stock of provisions; as it was, seeing that no more was to be had, they expressed their satisfaction by rubbing down their stomachs, and grunting in a manner which would have done credit to a herd of well-fed swine.

We were just arranging ourselves on the ground in a circle for the purpose of smoking and having a talk, "à la Indian," when a new party, with a large drove of horses and mules, made their appearance. These new-comers proved to be a small band of Americans, who were driving their cattle into the Eutaw country with the view of trading with that tribe of Indians. The owner of the animals and leader of the party was a Mr. Walker, an old acquaintance of Carson's. After securing his caballada, and making camp in our vicinity, Mr. Walker joined our party, and the interrupted council was resumed.

Though this was a state occasion, and one which required due gravity of countenance, I found it rather difficult to control my risibles at the singular scene which we presented.

Imagine us seated in a circle on the ground, checkered red and white, with here a half naked Indian, and there a mountaineer, almost as uncouth, in his own peculiar garb. The arms of both parties, though not ostentatiously displayed (which might have interfered with our negotiation), being placed where they could be reached at a moment's warning: a pipe (Carson's own particular "dudheen"), being put in requisition for the occasion, was duly filled with tobacco, lighted, and a short smoke having been taken by Carson, Walker and myself, it was then passed to the oldest man among our Indian guests, who took two or three long whiffs, retaining the smoke in his mouth, until his distorted face bore so strong a resemblance to an antiquated monkey's under trying circumstances, that I had all but disturbed the gravity of the assembly by bursting into a roar of laughter. The old warrior, having first reduced himself to the very verge of suffocation in his anxiety to make the most of the fragrant weed, then proceeded to utter a chorus of grunts, which were intended to signify his satisfaction either in meeting us, or, what is quite as likely, in the flavor of our tobacco. The pipe, having finally gone the rounds of our parti-colored circle, found its way back into the hands of the old Indian, who having placed it securely in his mouth, seemed to continue smoking in a fit of absence of mind, which not only induced him to refill it, but rendered him perfectly insensible to the reproving grunts of his brethren. I have since thought that the old warrior may have been a deep politician in his way, and therefore retained the pipe to obviate the necessity of his talking, which might have obliged him to commit himself disadvantageously upon some diplomatic question.

The talk then commenced. Kit told as much of his route and future intentions as he thought necessary, though I doubt whether they gained much *real* information; and concluded by charging divers murders and outrages upon the members of the tribe to which our visitors belonged. The Diggers answered to the effect that there were bad Indians living among the hills who did such things, but that for themselves they were perfectly innocent, never did anything wrong in their lives, entertained a great regard for the whites in general, and ourselves in particular; and wound up, diplomatically speaking, by "renewing to us the assurances of their distinguished consideration," coupled with a strong hint that a present (a horse, or some such trifle) would not be unacceptable as an evidence of our esteem.

These Digger Indians are by far the most degraded and miserable beings who inhabit this continent; their bag-like covering is of the very scantiest description, their food revolting; the puppies and rats of the Celestials being almost Epicurean when compared with a Pau-Eutaw bill of fare. Some of the parties which I have been mentioning brought lizards with them into our camp, and ate them raw, or with no further preparation than jerking off the reptile's tail. To obtain this description of food more readily, many of them carried with their arms a sort of hooked stick, not unlike a long cane, which they use in capturing them. The hair of these savages is long, reaching nearly to their middle, and almost as coarse as the mane of a mule. Their faces seem perfectly devoid of any intellectual expression, and—save the eye, which is exceedingly keen—their features are in nowise remarkable. The traveler can not but notice a strong similarity to a wild beast, both in their manners and appearance. I have repeatedly observed them turning the head from right to left quickly, while walking, in the manner of a prairie wolf. In voracity, they bear a greater resemblance to an anaconda than to a human being. I

have been told, by those who know them well, that
five or six of these Indians will sit round a dead
horse, and eat until nothing but the bones remain.
Unlike the tribes of the Rocky Mountains, they steal
your animals, not to ride, but to slaughter for food,
and a loss of this kind is rendered doubly provoking
to the trapper from the fact that they invariably
pick out your fattest and best conditioned stock. I
am informed, and I have no reason to disbelieve the
story, that they will even sell their own children
to the Californians, to obtain some addition to their
scanty supplies. It can not be denied that there is
some excuse for their failings in these respects; the
miserable country which they inhabit is incapable
of supporting them, and the surrounding tribes, who
occupy the more fertile portions of this region, look
upon these outcasts with a suspicious eye, and are
unrelenting in driving them from their hunting
grounds.

The arms of this degraded people consist of a bow
of uncommon length, and arrows headed with stone;
these last they are said to poison. In regard to their
mode of obtaining the venom for this purpose, I
have been told the following story, which, without
attempting to endorse, I shall relate as it was told
to me. The liquid which renders their shafts so
deadly is a combination of the rattlesnake's poison
with an extract which they distill from some plant

known only to themselves. This plant would appear to possess the qualities of the fabled Upas-tree, as the noisome vapors exhaled by distillation act so powerfully upon the procurer as to destroy life. It becomes therefore a matter of some moment to decide upon the individual who is to prepare the yearly stock of poison for his tribe. Now it would naturally be supposed that so dangerous an office would be shunned by all; but, on the contrary (says my narrator), a yearly contest takes place among the oldest squaws as to which shall receive the distinguished honor of sacrificing her life in the cause, and the conflict ends in the appointment of the successful competitor, who does the work and pays the penalty.

Our Indian visitors remained with us all day, hoping probably that some present would be given them; an expectation which was never destined to be fulfilled. About sunset, Kit's usual cry of "Catch up!" warned us to prepare for the road; and while most of the men were engaged in packing the animals, a young Indian (who, by the way, had been among the loudest in his protestations of goodwill) seized the opportunity to abstract from the luggage of an old mountaineer a tin cup, which he tossed across the creek into the long rushes fringing its banks. Now this act, although certainly a gross violation of the laws of hospitality, was, under the circumstances of the case, a most ingenious mode of

stealing, as the cup, even if it had been missed amid
the hurry of our departure, would have been supposed to be accidentally lost; and the almost naked
savages, who had evidently no means of concealing
it about their persons, relieved from any suspicion
of dishonesty. As it happened, I was the only one
who perceived the manœuvre, and calling the man to
whom the cup belonged, I informed him of his loss,
at the same time pointing out the offender. He was,
as I have already remarked, an old mountaineer,
and long experience among the Indians had taught
him the best course to pursue; so without wasting
time and words in expostulation, he grasped the dis-
honest warrior by the hair with one hand and round
the leg with the other, and then plunged him, head
first, into the creek, at the same time ordering him,
under penalty of death, to swim across, find the cup,
and return it. This the savage did, though with
evident reluctance; and as he stood dripping upon
the bank, I thought that I had never seen a more
forlorn or crest-fallen looking creature. As for his
companions, so far from expressing any indignation at his treatment, they seemed to look upon the
whole affair as a good joke, and laughed heartily.

Shortly after our departure from this encampment, we perceived smoke rising from prominent
hills in our vicinity;—these smokes were repeated at
various points along our route, showing that the

Diggers, for some purpose best known to themselves, thought fit to apprise their tribe of our passage through the country. During the following day, parties of these Indians showed themselves occasionally upon the crests of inaccessible hills, but seemed unwilling to come within gun-shot: nor was it until we had gone two days' journey from the camp where they had attempted to steal, that a few of their people mustered courage to visit us. And when they did so, the actions of the party were so suspicious that Kit concluded to retain one of their number (a young warrior about eighteen years of age) as a sort of hostage for their good behavior during the night. Our so doing appeared to give much greater uneasiness to the tribe than to the object of their solicitude, who either from a feeling of security, or by a strong exercise of that power of self-control for which the North American Indian is famous, exhibited no signs of timidity, but made himself perfectly at home after his own fashion. Sitting beside us on the ground, he conversed freely with Carson in the low, guttural accents of his native tongue, which he eked out with gestures and figures rudely drawn upon the ground. After partaking of our supper, he stretched himself quietly upon a blanket which we had lent him for his bed, and was about composing himself to sleep when his companions set up a most dismal howling from the adjoining hills. This yelling—sounding more like a chorus of screech-owls, or a troop of hungry wolves, than anything else I can compare it to—was rendered doubly mournful by the gloomy shades of evening, and the otherwise total silence of the hour. This disturbance was finally quieted by Kit's replying in the Pau-Eutaw tongue, aided by the assurances of the young man himself, who yelled back an answer to the effect that he was still in the land of the living. We knew too well the treacherous character of these people to permit this Indian to sleep in our very midst without some guard over his movements during the night: so our own mess divided this duty among them. It fell to my lot to keep the first watch until midnight; and I remember well standing beside our temporary captive with my rifle in my hand, almost envying the calmness with which he slumbered, although separated from his friends, and surrounded by those whom he must have considered the natural enemies of his race. I must not forget to say that, while arranging his bed, he asked for his bow and arrows, which I handed him; these he placed carefully beneath the blanket by his side, explaining to me, by signs, that the damp might impair their efficacy by relaxing the bowstring, which was composed of twisted sinews.

The night passed quietly away; and in the morning we allowed our hostage to depart, making him a

few trifling presents as a recompense for his in-
voluntary detention. Among these matters, an old
pair of pantaloons, worn and tattered from long

DIGGER INDIAN.

service, seemed most valued by their new possessor.
So much was he elated by this acquisition, that it
seemed difficult for him to restrain the expression
of his joy. In fact, no city dandy, faultlessly arrayed
for the fashionable side of Broadway, could have
exhibited more perfect satisfaction in his strut and

air than our untutored Digger. I doubt not that his new costume made him the wonder and envy of his comrades, whose principal garb was the dress with which Dame Nature had provided them.

CHAPTER III

FROM THE ARCHILETTE TO LITTLE SALT LAKE

Fuentes and Hernandez—Revenge of Carson and Godey—
Arrival at the Rio Virgen—Scene of Tabeau's death—
Archambeau shoots a Digger—Las Vegas de Santa
Clara.

AT the Archilette, a well-known camping-ground
in the desert, we passed a day and night. This
dreary spot has obtained a mournful notoriety
among the few travelers through these sandy wastes,
from its having been the theatre of a tragedy which,
though I have heard the tale from the lips of Carson
himself, and witnessed the bleaching bones of the
victims, I will relate in the words of Frémont, who
has given in his journal full details of the outrage.
The Colonel first mentions it under date of April
24th, 1844, when he says:

"In the afternoon we were surprised by the sudden
appearance in the camp of two Mexicans—a man and
a boy. The name of the man was Andreas Fuentes;
and that of the boy (a handsome lad, eleven years
old) Pablo Hernandez. They belonged to a party
consisting of six persons, the remaining four being

the wife of Fuentes, the father and mother of Pablo,
and Santiago Giacome, a resident of New Mexico, with
a cavalcade of about thirty horses; they had come
out from Pueblo de Los Angeles, near the coast, to
travel more at leisure, and obtain better grass. Having
advanced as far into the desert as was considered con-
sistent with their safety, they halted at the Archilette,
one of the customary camping grounds, about eighty
miles from our encampment, where there is a spring
of good water, with sufficient grass, and concluded
to await there the arrival of the great caravan. Several
Indians were soon discovered lurking about the camp,
who, in a day or two after, came in, and after behaving
in a very friendly manner, took their leave, without
awakening any suspicions. Their deportment begat
a security which proved fatal. In a few days afterward, suddenly a party of about one hundred Indians
appeared in sight, advancing toward the camp. It was
too late, or they seemed not to have presence of mind
to take proper measures of safety; and the Indians
charged down into their camp, shouting as they advanced, and discharging flights of arrows. Pablo and
Fuentes were on horse-guard at the time, and mounted
according to the custom of the country. One of the
principal objects of the Indians was to get possession
of the horses, and part of them immediately surrounded the band; but in obedience to the shouts of
Giacome, Fuentes drove the animals over and through
the assailants, in spite of their arrows; and, abandoning the rest to their fate, carried them off at speed
across the plain. Knowing that they would be pursued
by the Indians, without making any halt, except to

shift their saddles to other horses, they drove them on
for about sixty miles, and this morning left them at
a watering-place upon the trail called Agua de Tomaso.
Without giving themselves any time for rest, they
hurried on, hoping to meet the Spanish caravan, when
they discovered my camp. I received them kindly,
taking them into my own mess, and promised them
such aid as circumstances might put it in my power
to give.''

Under date of April 25th Colonel Frémont again
alludes to the subject, in the following extract from
his journal:

"After traveling about twenty-five miles we arrived
at the Agua de Tomaso—the spring where the horses
had been left; but as we expected, they were gone.
A brief examination of the ground convinced us that
they had been driven off by the Indians. Carson and
Godey volunteered with the Mexican to pursue them;
and, well mounted, the three set off on the trail. In
the evening Fuentes returned, his horse having failed;
but Carson and Godey had continued the pursuit. In
the afternoon of the next day, a war-whoop was heard,
such as Indians make when returning from a victorious
enterprise; and soon Carson and Godey appeared,
driving before them a band of horses, recognized by
Fuentes to be part of those they had lost. Two bloody
scalps dangling from the end of Godey's gun announced that they had overtaken the Indians as well
as the horses. They informed us that, after Fuentes
left them from the failure of his horse, they continued
the pursuit alone, and toward nightfall entered the

mountains, into which the trail led. After sunset the moon gave light, and they followed the trail by moonshine until late in the night, when it entered a narrow defile, and was difficult to follow. Afraid of losing it in the darkness of the defile, they tied up their horses, struck no fire, and lay down to sleep in silence and in darkness. Here they lay from midnight till morning. At daylight they resumed the pursuit, and about sunrise discovered the horses; and immediately dismounting and tying up their own, they crept cautiously to a rising ground which intervened, from the crest of which they perceived the encampment of four lodges close by. They proceeded quietly and had got within thirty or forty yards of their object, when a movement among the horses discovered them to the Indians. Giving the war-shout, they instantly charged into the camp, regardless of the number which the four lodges would imply. The Indians received them with a flight of arrows shot from their long bows, one of which passed through Godey's shirt collar barely missing his neck; our men fired their rifles upon a steady aim, and rushed in. Two Indians were stretched upon the ground, fatally pierced with bullets; the rest fled, except a lad that was captured. The scalps of the fallen were instantly stripped off; but in the process, one of them, who had two balls through his body, sprang to his feet, the blood streaming from his skinned head, and uttered a hideous howl. An old squaw, possibly his mother, stopped and looked back from the mountain side she was climbing, threatening and lamenting. The frightful spectacle appalled the stout hearts of our men; but they did what humanity required, and quickly terminated the agonies of the gory savage. They were now masters of the camp, which was a pretty little recess in the mountain, with a fine spring, and apparently safe from all invasion. Great preparations had been made to feast a large party, for it was a very proper place for a rendezvous, and for the celebration of such orgies as robbers of the desert would delight in. Several of the best horses had been killed, skinned, and cut up; for the Indians, living in mountains, and only coming into the plains to rob and murder, make no other use of horses than to eat them. Large earthen vessels were on the fire, boiling and stewing the horse-beef; and several baskets, containing fifty or sixty pairs of moccasins, indicated the presence, or expectation, of a considerable party. They released the boy who had given strong evidence of the stoicism, or something else, of the savage character, in commencing his breakfast upon a horse's head, as soon as he found he was not to be killed, but only tied as a prisoner. Their object accomplished, our men gathered up all the surviving horses, fifteen in number, returned upon their trail, and rejoined us at our camp in the afternoon of the same day. They had rode about one hundred miles in the pursuit and return, and all in thirty hours. The time, place, object, and numbers considered, this expedition of Carson and Godey may be considered among the boldest and most disinterested which the annals of Western adventure, so full of daring deeds, can present. Two men, in a savage desert, pursue day and night an unknown body of Indians, into the defiles of an un-known mountain—attack them on sight, without count-

ing numbers—and defeat them in an instant, and for
what? To punish the robbers of the desert, and to
avenge the wrongs of Mexicans whom they did not
know. I repeat, it was Carson and Godey who did
this—the former an American born in the Boon's
Lick county of Missouri; the latter a Frenchman,
born in St. Louis; and both trained to Western enterprise from early life.''

Under date of April 29th the same writer adds:

''To-day we had to reach the Archilette, distant
seven miles, where the Mexican party had been
attacked; and leaving our encampment, we traversed
a part of the desert, the most sterile and repulsive
that we had yet seen. Our course was generally
north; and after crossing an intervening ridge, we
descended into a sandy plain, or basin, in the middle
of which was the grassy spot, with its springs and
willow bushes, which constitutes a camping place in
the desert, and is called the Archilette. The dead
silence of the place was ominous; and galloping
rapidly up, we found only the corpses of the two
men; everything else was gone. They were naked,
mutilated, and pierced with arrows. Hernandez had
evidently fought, and with desperation. He lay in
advance of the willow, half facing the tent which
sheltered his family, as if he had come out to meet
danger, and to repulse it from that asylum. One of
his hands, and both his legs, had been cut off. Giacome,
who was a large and strong-looking man, was lying
in one of the willow shelters, pierced with arrows. Of
the women no trace could be found, and it was evi-

dent they had been carried off captive. A little lap-dog, which had belonged to Pablo's mother, remained with the dead bodies, and was frantic with joy at seeing Pablo; he, poor child, was frantic with grief; and filled the air with lamentations for his father and mother. *"Mi padre! mi madre!"* was his incessant cry. When we beheld this pitiable sight, and pictured to ourselves the fate of the two women, carried off by savages so brutal and so loathsome, all compunction for the scalped-alive Indians ceased; and we rejoiced that Carson and Godey had been able to give so useful a lesson to these American Arabs, who lie in wait to murder and plunder the innocent traveler. We were all too much affected by the sad feelings which the place inspired, to remain an unnecessary moment. The night we were obliged to pass there. Early in the morning we left it, having first written a brief account of what had happened, and put it in the cleft of a pole planted at the spring, that the approaching caravan might learn the fate of their friends. In commemoration of the event we called the place *Agua de Hernandez*—Hernandez's Spring."

As I have remarked, the foregoing details were narrated to me by Carson, one of the principal actors in the affair, while we were encamped upon the ground where the murders were committed. I remember that during our visit the dreariness of the scene was enhanced by a coming storm, which rendered the sides of the naked *sierras* still darker, and muttered solemnly among the hills. The bones of

the unfortunate men still whitened on the sand, and
one of the skulls which the Indians had thrust upon
a pole planted in the ground, betokened the recent
presence of their murderers.

Upon reaching the banks of the Rio Virgen (Virgin's River), we found the "Indian Sign," as it is
called by the trappers, growing everywhere more
plentiful. The signal fires, too, were still continued;
and furnished additional evidence that our presence
in this region was regarded with suspicion and distrust. Among our halts near the Virgen, we stopped
at the point where Frémont, in the spring of 1844,
lost one of his best men, an old mountaineer, who fell
a victim to the hostility of these same Indians. The
intrepid explorer has thus described his murder in
his official report; from which valuable document I
have already taken the liberty of quoting.

Under date of May 9th, 1844, he writes:

"I had been engaged in arranging plants; and,
fatigued with the heat of the day, I fell asleep in the
afternoon, and did not awake until sundown. Presently Carson came to me, and reported that Tabeau,
who early in the day had left his post, and, without
my knowledge, rode back to the camp we had left, in
search of a lame mule, had not returned. While we
were speaking, a smoke rose suddenly from the cottonwood grove below, which plainly told us what had
befallen him; it was raised to inform the surrounding
Indians that a blow had been struck, and to tell them

to be on their guard. Carson, with several men, well mounted, was instantly sent down the river, but returned in the night, without tidings of the missing man. They went to the camp we had left, but neither he nor the mule was there. Searching down the river, they found the tracks of the mule, evidently driven along by Indians, whose tracks were on each side of those made by the animal. After going several miles, they came to the mule itself, standing in some bushes, mortally wounded in the side by an arrow, and left to die, that it might be afterward butchered for food. They also found, in another place, as they were hunting about on the ground for Tabeau's tracks, something that looked like a little puddle of blood, but which the darkness prevented them from verifying. With these details, they returned to our camp, and their report saddened all our hearts.''

"*May* 10*th*.—This morning, as soon as there was light enough to follow tracks, I set out myself, with Mr. Fitzpatrick and several men, in search of Tabeau. We went to the spot where the appearance of puddled blood had been seen; and this, we saw at once, had been the place where he fell and died. Blood upon the leaves, and beaten-down bushes, showed that he had got his wound about twenty paces from where he fell, and that he had struggled for his life. He had probably been shot through the lungs with an arrow. From the place where he lay and bled, it could be seen that he had been dragged to the river's bank and thrown into it. No vestige of what had belonged to him could be found, except a fragment of his horse equipment. Horse, gun, clothes—all became the prey of these

Arabs of the New World. Tabeau had been one of our best men, and his unhappy death spread a gloom over our party. Men who have gone through such dangers and sufferings as we had seen, become like brothers, and feel each other's loss. To defend and avenge each other, is the deep feeling of all.''

As an apology for this long quotation, I may state that many of our party had been friends and companions of the unfortunate Tabeau; and the exciting sensations, called up by revisiting the scene of his tragic end, found vent in the deep and general feelings of indignation expressed by our mountaineers against the tribe who had committed the murder.

We had scarcely been encamped two hours, when one of the horse-guard reported that he discovered fresh Indian tracks near our caballada, and expressed the opinion that they had just been made by some Digger spy, who had reconnoitred our position with the view of stealing the animals. With the associations connected with the spot, it will hardly seem wonderful that our line of conduct was soon determined upon. Carson, two old hunters named Auchambeau and Lewis, and myself, took our guns, and started upon the freshly-made trail. The foot-tracks at first led us through the winding paths, along the river bottom, where we were obliged to travel in Indian file; and then turned suddenly aside, ascending one of the steep sand hills which bordered upon the stream. There we lost some time from the obscurity of the trail, but finally recovered it upon the crest of the bluff. A moment after, I heard Kit shouting, ''There he goes''; and looking in the direction to which he pointed, I saw a Digger with his bow and arrows at his back, evidently badly frightened, and running for his life. Such traveling through deep sand I never saw before. The fellow bounded like a deer, swinging himself from side to side, so as to furnish a very uncertain mark for our rifles. Once, he seemed inclined to tarry, and take a shot at us; but after an attempt to draw his bow, he concluded that he had no time to waste, and hurried on. Kit fired first, and, for a wonder, missed him; but it was a long shot, and on the wing to boot. I tried him next with a musket, sending two balls and six buck-shot after him, with like success. Auchambeau followed me, with no better fortune; and we had begun to think the savage bore a charmed life, when Lewis, who carried a long Missouri rifle, dropped upon one knee, exclaiming, ''I'll bring him, boys.'' By this time the Indian was nearly two hundred yards distant, and approaching the edge of a steep cañon (as it is called) of rocks and sand. The thing was now getting exciting, and we watched the man with almost breathless care, as Lewis fired; at the crack of his rifle the Digger bounded forward, and his arm, which had been raised in the air, fell suddenly to his side. He had evidently been hit through or near the shoulder; yet, strange to say, such is their knowledge of the country, and so great their power of endurance, that he succeeded in making his escape. In running, this warrior (who may have been an inferior chief) dropped his head-dress of fur; which, as he did not stop to get it, I thought might fairly come under the head of captured property, and took it away accordingly. From this time forward we had no more trouble with the Diggers.

Our adventures in the desert were eventually terminated by our arrival at Las Vegas de Santa Clara, and a pleasant thing it was to look once more upon green grass and sweet water, and to reflect that the dreariest portion of our journey lay behind us, so that the sands and jornadas of the great basin would weary our tired animals no more. But with all this, dangers, hardships, and privations were yet to be encountered and overcome; the craggy steeps and drifted snows of the Wah-Satch and Rocky Mountains, with many a turbid stream and rapid river, presented obstacles of no small magnitude to our onward progress. But with a better country before us, and the cool mountain breezes to fan our fevered limbs, we looked forward with stout hearts to the future, doubting not that we should yet attain our journey's end.

Las Vegas de Santa Clara, to the traveler going eastward, must always appear beautiful by comparison. The noise of running water, the large grassy meadows, from which the spot takes its name, and the green hills which circle it round—all tend to captivate the eye and please the senses of the way-worn *voyageur*.

CHAPTER IV

FROM LITTLE SALT LAKE TO THE GRAND RIVER

Meeting with Eutaws—Wacarra—An Indian trencherman
—And a skillful horse-trader—A gift to Wacarra's
squaw—Over the Wah-Satch—Mules' first experience with snow—Camping in the snow—Fishing with
arrows and with sticks—Fate of the seven Arkansaw
travelers—Crossing Grand River—The raft—The
upset—Loss of arms and provisions.

IF I remember rightly, it was not far from the
Little Salt Lake that we first met with the Eutaw
Indians. At this point we found one of their principal chiefs, "Wacarra," or Walker, as he is commonly called by the Americans. His encampment
consisted of four lodges, inhabited by his wives,
children, and suite of inferior warriors and chiefs.
This party was awaiting the coming of the great
Spanish caravan, from whom they intended taking
the yearly tribute which the tribe exact as the
price of a safe-conduct through their country. I
found a vast difference in all respects between these
Indians and the miserable beings whom we had
hitherto seen. The Eutaws are perhaps the most
powerful and warlike tribe now remaining upon this

continent. They appear well provided with fire-
arms, which they are said to use with the precision
of veteran riflemen. I remember they expressed
their surprise that the white men should use so much
powder in firing at a mark, while to them every load
brought a piece of game or the scalp of an enemy.
Wacarra (or Walker, as I shall call him) received
our party very graciously; in fact, their attentions,
so far at least as my humble self was concerned,
became rather overpowering, as the sequel will show.

We had been riding hard, and, as I have before
stated, our rations were both poor and scanty. But
to eat is a necessity; and when food is prepared,
to secure your own individual share, even under such
circumstances, becomes a duty of considerable importance. As our encampment was not over a hundred yards distant from the lodges of our Indian
neighbors, we had scarcely sat down to take breakfast—it ought to have been called dinner, as it was
then near noon, and we had eaten nothing since the
day before—when Walker's warriors joined us.
Now it is a difficult matter for me to eat a meal
in comfort when even a dog looks wistfully in my
face; and I sat gazing in some perplexity, first upon
the tin platter which contained my share of the
atole, and then at the capacious mouth of a burly
chieftain who stood evidently waiting for an invitation to sit down. At length I mustered my courage,

and by various signs, which he appeared to have no difficulty in comprehending, tendered a gracious invitation to my red-skinned friend to join me, and taste the *atole*. Now before inviting my guest I had fully determined upon the line of conduct which it would be necessary for me to pursue, to obtain anything like a fair proportion of the meal. My plan was this: I intended to try my pewter teaspoon, with which I hoped to consume the *atole* faster than my copper-colored friend, should he eat with the long sharp knife which I had destined for his use, fondly trusting that he would cut his mouth if he attempted to handle it rapidly. I have since thought that Mr. Eutaw saw through the whole design, for, as he commenced operations, he favored me with an indescribable look and grunt, at the same time turning the knife in his hand so as to manage it with its back toward him. I saw in a moment that my chances were small, and quickness of execution everything. But it was no use; as the Western men say, I was "no whar." I worked away with my teaspoon until the perspiration fairly streamed from my forehead, bolting the hot *atole* like a salamander, but all would not do; the Indian, with his broad-bladed knife, took three mouthfuls to my one, and, hang the fellow! even condescended to look at me occasionally in a patronizing sort of way, and nod his head encouragingly. The solid portion of

my repast soon grew "beautifully less," but before
it had entirely disappeared, the Eutaw grasped the
plate, and passed it to a friend of his, who stood
directly behind him. This fellow literally *licked* the
plate clean, and without any relaxation of his almost
stoical gravity, turned it upside down, at the same
time uttering a significant grunt, as an intimation
that a further supply would be acceptable. I looked
ruefully at the empty dish, but the dark eyes of my
guest were intently regarding me, and I had no
time for meditation. So with a desperate determination to do nothing by halves, I handed my large
coffee cup, with its precious contents, to the chief,
at the same time smiling as amiably as my experiences would permit. Now this cup of coffee was my
last and greatest dependence, as I knew that nothing was to be had in the way of eatables until the
following day, and a long ride lay before us. So it
was with something more than nervous trepidation
that I watched the savage put the cup to his lips.
Here, too, I was buoyed up by a delusive hope: certainly, thought I, he can not like coffee; the sugar
is almost gone, and the beverage so bitter, that I
hardly fancy it myself, and this fellow ought to spit
it out in abhorrence. I watch his movements with
breathless anxiety—he tastes—gives a grunt of uncertainty, and without lowering the cup, turns his
eye to me, to ask if it is good. I shake my head

negatively—could I have spoken his guttural jargon, I would have made a most impressive speech, to the effect that coffee was a great medicine, harmless to the paleface, but certain death to Indians in general and Eutaws in particular. But, alas! my sign was either unheeded or misunderstood. I sat in speechless agony, while the bottom of the cup was gradually elevated in the air, till—just as I was about commencing an expostulation, my guest uttered a satisfied sigh, and passed the cup to the same person who had cleared the platter. It was all gone—I felt it. Yes; "before you could say Jack Robinson" the second Indian had finished it, grounds and all, and placed the cup, bottom up, upon the ground. My meal for the day was gone; and I felt that to ask sympathy would only call forth a laugh against myself. So I kept my sorrows within my own breast until some days afterward, when Kit thought it one of the best jokes he had ever heard.

I have fancied that we must have reached Little Salt Lake upon one of my unlucky days, for it seems that I was destined to be cheated in a horse-trade by the same Indian who had consumed my breakfast.

The reader will probably remember my description of the horse which I purchased in California, and which I have alluded to as an animal of terrible experiences. I had found him so worthless upon the route that he had scarcely been ridden; and now the sharp stones of the desert had injured his hoofs so seriously that I knew it would be impossible to bring him over the rugged country which remained to be crossed. Accordingly, I had the miserable beast duly paraded, and having got him in such a position that a rock at his back prevented him from lying down, a thing not to be desired until the negotiation for his transfer was ended, I proceeded, by means of signs and the few words of Eutaw which I had learned, to open a treaty for his exchange. My Indian friends, after carefully examining the animal, sent a boy for the horse which they wished to give for him. Pending the return of their messenger, they employed the time in destroying what little of good character my poor steed had ever possessed, shook their heads despondingly over his battered hoofs, and grunted hideously in token of their strong disapprobation.

The perfection of horse-flesh (which, alas! was soon to come into my stock) now made his appearance in the shape of a rough-looking Indian pony, who might have been twenty years of age or upward; his Eutaw groom led him by a hair rope, which he had twisted round his nose; but upon a signal from the chief the lad scrambled upon the animal's back, and began putting the old veteran through his paces, which seemed limited to a one-sided walk, and a gallop which would have done

credit to a wounded buffalo bull. As a last induce-
ment they exhibited his hoofs, which certainly looked
hard enough, in all conscience. After considerable
hesitation I was about making the trade upon equal
terms, when to my great disgust the chief informed
me that he could not think of parting with so valuable an animal, unless I gave him some present to
boot. This new demand I was fain to comply with,
and parted not only with my broken-down horse, but
with one of my two Mexican blankets; and many
was the time while chilled by the cold breezes of the
Rocky Mountains that I thought, with a shiver, of
my horse-trade by the Little Salt Lake.

Before leaving this encampment, I was invited
by Walker to visit his lodge, and accompanied him
accordingly. These lodges are made of skins sewed
together, with an opening at the top which serves
as a chimney for the smoke, the fire being built on
the ground in the centre of the lodge. Upon entering the lodge the children crowded round me, ad-
miring the gaudy scarlet cloth with which my
leathern hunting-shirt was lined; most of these
young people were armed with small bows and
arrows which they amused themselves by aiming at
me. Walker's wife, or wives, for I think he had
several, were busied in their domestic avocations
about the lodge, and one of them (a good-looking
squaw of some eighteen or twenty years, who seemed

CAMP AMONG THE WAH-SATCH MOUNTAINS.

to be the favorite), was kind enough to spread a deer-skin for my accommodation. Wishing to repay her courtesy, I called my servant Juan, and directed him to get a brass breast-plate with the letters "U.S." conspicuously displayed, which I had among my traps, polish it up, and bring it to me. This he did, and I shall never forget the joy of this belle of the wilderness, upon receiving the shining metal. With the aid of a small mirror, which had probably been obtained from some passing trader, she arranged the breast-plate (fully two inches square) upon her raven locks, and then, with the air of a tragedy queen, marched up and down in front of the lodge, looking with great contempt upon her envious companions. It was certainly an amusing scene, and goes to prove that vanity may exist as strongly in the character of a Eutaw squaw, as in the breast of a city belle; with this difference perhaps, that it is exhibited with much less taste among those whose education should have taught them better things.

After leaving the Little Salt Lake, we traveled over or near the Wah-Satch Mountains for several days, meeting with few adventures worthy of note until we reached the mountain snows, which even in the month of June we found several feet in depth. Some of our mules, who had never seen snow before —having been reared among the sunny plains of

California—showed great uneasiness upon first approaching it; they would stop, try the depth of the drift with their hoofs, and hesitate until fairly spurred into it by their riders. Upon the mountain tops we sometimes encamped upon snow heaps many feet in depth, and while thus situated my mode of

UTAH LODGE.

protecting myself from the cold during the night was as follows. I made a small excavation in the side of some drift least exposed to the wind, and then wrapping myself closely in my solitary blanket, I spread my saddle cloths beneath me, and rolled myself into the hole, where I managed to sleep pretty comfortably, even amid the snows of the Wah-Satch Mountains.

In this same section of country, we encamped one evening upon a beautiful little lake situated in a hollow among the mountains, but at so great an elevation that it was, even in summer, surrounded by snow, and partially covered with ice. There we were again visited by the Eutaw Indians, who, as usual, behaved in a very friendly manner. Our provisions had now become so scanty that it was

SLEEPING IN THE SNOW.

necessary to add to our stock by purchasing what we could from the Indians. From the party who here visited us, we managed to obtain a portion of a Rocky Mountain sheep, or "big-horn," as it is often called;—and, upon Kit's asking for fish, one of the Indians departed, but in a few minutes returned with a fine trout, which we bought for a couple of charges of powder. Our bargain had hardly been placed upon the fire when we discovered that the fish had been killed by an arrow-wound in the back. While we were wondering at this novel

mode of taking trout, two of our men came into
camp with as many fish as they could carry, and
told us that they had caught as many more, but
left them upon the banks of the lake. It seemed that
in wandering about, they had discovered a little
stream, a tributary to the lake, but quite shallow;
this stream they represented as swarming with fish,
so that they had gone in and killed them with sticks.
To our hungry people this was *more* than good news;
and that evening was devoted to the composition
of a chowder, which was literally fish *"au naturel."*

Our supper ended, it was unanimously decided
that we should move our camp next day no further
than the stream, where we contemplated spending
the day in fishing. With this pleasant expectation
I betook myself to bed, where I was soon lulled to
sleep by a low, monotonous strain which one of our
Indian guests amused himself by singing.

By sunrise next morning we were not only settled
in our new camp, but up to our knees in the icy
water in pursuit of its frightened tenants. If fish
keep chronicles, I fancy that those in the waters of
Trout Lake will not soon forget us; for such a
slaughter of the finny tribe I have rarely seen. For
my own part, with an old bayonet fastened to a stick,
I caught five dozen—and a twinge of rheumatism,
which reminds me of the circumstance even now.

With our former experiences of scanty rations and

hard travel, it will scarcely be thought surprising
that after a day's rest and our famous feast of
chowder, we should feel as if we could have faced
not only a whole legion of Diggers, but the "Old
Boy" himself (always supposing that the "Evil
One" could haunt so cold a region as the Wah-Satch
Mountains). Our course was now for the most part
upward; sometimes crossing snowy ridges, where the
icy winds made us fairly crouch in our saddles; and
then descending into valleys where the pine-forests
afforded a grateful shelter from the sun.

While traversing one of these gorges, we came
suddenly upon seven human skeletons, six of which,
bleached by the elements, lay scattered here and
there, where the bones had been dragged by hungry
wolves along a space of some yards in extent; the
seventh, which, from its less accessible position,
being sheltered by rocks, and, in part, by a fallen
tree, had remained undisturbed by beasts of prey,
seemed extended where its owner died. Upon a further examination of the ground, we concluded that
these mournful relics were the remains of some unfortunate party of whites or Mexicans who had been
cut off by the Indians. The skeleton which lay alone
appeared, from the arrow heads and bullets yet
marking the tree which guarded it, to have belonged
to an individual of the party who had fought from
this shelter until overcome by superior numbers.

These surmises afterward proved but too true, as we learned from a band of friendly Eutaws, who reported that the bones which we had discovered were those of a party of Americans from Arkansas, who had been surprised by hostile Indians while resting at noon, and instantly killed, with the exception of one of their number, who snatched up his rifle, retreated to the nearest cover, and there battled with all the energy of despair, killing two of the savages before being dispatched by the arrows of his assailants. It was a sad sight for us to gaze upon these mouldering fragments. None of us could say at what moment their fate might be ours—to die amid the wilderness, far from friends and home, with the wolf to howl over us, and the wild mountain breezes to chant our requiem, as they roared through the sombre branches of the pines. How many sad hearts may have yearned, and how many bright eyes, filled with tears, of the sufferers from "hope deferred," who were yet looking for the brothers and husbands whose fate we had been the first to learn!

I remember celebrating my birthday, which comes in June (the precise date I will leave the reader to guess, if he be a Yankee), by standing upon the banks of Grand River, and looking with a most rueful countenance and many secret forebodings upon the turbid current of the swollen stream. And

well I might. I have said it was in June; and one
might suppose that a cold-bath in early summer was
no great hardship; but in this case, I found that
the association of the month with summer ended
with its name; for the strong wind felt more like
a December blast as it went rushing by, and the
angry torrent at my feet, fed by the melting snows,
was many degrees colder than the water of a mountain spring. But this formidable obstacle was to
be passed, and how to overcome the difficulty I
scarcely knew. Kit, however, solved the problem,
by proposing a raft, and accordingly all hands went
to work with a will to collect the necessary material
from the neighboring woods. Kit, in his shirt-
sleeves, working hard himself—instructing here and
directing there, and as usual, proving himself the
master-spirit of the party. After much labor, a few
logs were properly cut, notched, and rolled into the
water, where they were carefully fastened together
by binding them with our *réatas,* until this rude expedient furnished a very passable mode of convey-
ance for a light load of luggage.

Having freighted it as heavily as we dared with
our packs and riding saddles, and placed the bags
containing the California mails upon the securest
portion, we next proceeded to determine who of our
party should be the first to swim the stream. Five
men were at length selected, and as I was a good

swimmer I concluded to join the expedition as captain. So taking Auchambeau as my first mate, we two plunged into the stream; and having arranged our men at their appointed stations, only waited Kit's final orders, to trust ourselves to the waters. These instructions were soon briefly given in the following words, "All you men who can't swim may hang on to the corners of the raft, but don't any of you try to get upon it except Auchambeau, who has the pole to guide it with; those of you who can swim are to get hold of the tow-line, and pull it along; keep a good lookout for rocks and floating timber; and whatever you do, don't lose the mail bags." And now with one sturdy shove, our frail support was fairly launched, and with a farewell cheer from our comrades upon the shore we consigned ourselves to the mercy of the tide.

I have remarked that I went as captain; but once under way, I found that we were all captains; if indeed giving orders did any good where half one's words were lost amid the roaring of the rapids. In fact we mismanaged the business altogether, until at length I fancy that the poor stream, already vexed beyond endurance, determined to take the matter under its own guidance, out of pity for the nautical ignorance which we had displayed; and finally settled the thing by abandoning us in disgust upon the same side from whence we had started, but more than a mile further down. Ere this operation was concluded, however, it favored me, doubtless in consideration of my captainship, with a parting token; which but for the ready aid of Auchambeau must have finished my adventures upon the spot. I had swam out with a lariat to secure the unfortunate raft to a tree, when the current brought the heavy mass of timber into violent contact with my breast, throwing me back senseless into the channel. Just as I was performing a final feat, in the way of going down, Auchambeau got hold of my hair, which I luckily wore long, and dragged me out upon the bank, where I came to in due course of time.

Our situation was now far from pleasant, the only article of dress which we wore being our hats, the rest of our clothing having been left behind to come by another raft. To go up the rapids against the stream was out of the question; and to cross from where we were, with a considerable fall and jagged rocks just below us, equally impossible. So we had no resource but to shoulder our baggage and travel back on foot, following, as nearly as the thickets would permit, the windings of the river; and uttering more than one anathema upon the thorny plants, which wounded our unprotected feet at every step. It was high noon before we reached camp; and nearly four o'clock ere we

BUILDING A RAFT

were again prepared, and once more summoned up our resolution for a new trial.

This second attempt, after an infinite deal of trouble, proved successful, and we landed upon the opposite bank in a state of almost utter exhaustion; indeed Auchambeau, from over-exertion, and long exposure to the chilling snow water, was taken, upon reaching the shore, with cramps which convulsed him so terribly that we feared they might even destroy life itself. Our first care was, therefore, for him; and by dint of violent friction and rolling in the sand we succeeded in restoring our patient; and then turned our attention to unloading the raft, which had been partly drawn out of the river, and secured to the trunk of a fallen cotton-wood. In this labor we were assisted by a party of Eutaw Indians who had come down to meet us. In fact these fellows did the greater portion of the work, as our weary crew were as yet incapable of much exertion. I have since thought that while thus employed we must have looked like Robinson Crusoe, and his man Friday, supposing those distinguished individuals to have been multiplied by five; the wild scenery, the dashing waters, and our own singular costumes (for we were by this time dressed in buffalo robes borrowed from our Indian friends), all combining to carry out the delusion.

Having seen our baggage safely landed, and beheld

the raft (bad luck to it, for in this instance I could not "speak well of the bridge which carried me over") go down the rapids, to be dashed against the rocky cliffs below, we ascended the stream, hallooing to our companions to notify them of our safe arrival; the receipt of which information they acknowledged by a hearty cheer. Both parties, with the assistance of the Indians, then prepared to cross our caballada, who were expected to swim the river. With this view we selected a point upon our side, considerably below the position occupied by the opposite party, where the bank shelved gradually, and afforded a better footing than elsewhere. Here we took our station to attract the attention of the swimming animals by shouting and whistling. Upon our signifying our readiness to receive them, one of the opposite party rode into the water upon the old bell-mare, and the frightened mules were forced to follow, urged on by the yells and blows of their drivers. In a few moments the whole caballada was under way; the old bell-mare, striking out and breasting the waves gallantly, while the mules, with only their heads and long ears visible above the water, came puffing like small high-pressure steamboats in her wake. The yelling on our side now commenced, in which concert the Indians took the thorough base, performing to admiration; while our Mexican muleteers rent the air with their favorite cry of *"anda mula," "hupar mula."* The animals, attracted by the noise, made straight for us; and we soon had the gratification of seeing them safely landed, dripping and shaking themselves like so many Newfoundland dogs.

At this point, however, our good fortune was destined to end. Kit, it is true, with a few men, and a small portion of luggage, made the passage safely; but a large raft, which carried the greater share of our provisions, was dashed against a sawyer in the stream, which separated the logs, leaving the men to save themselves as they best could; this they did with considerable difficulty; but six rifles, three saddles, much of the ammunition, and nearly all our provisions were totally lost. Under these depressing circumstances, our camp that night was anything but a lively one; the Eutaws being the only persons who seemed to feel like laughing. Indeed, I half think that our loss put them in high good-humor, as they had some prospect of recovering the rifles, when a lower stage of water should enable them to explore the bed of the stream. The little that remained of our private mess stores, was now the only certain dependence left to us in the way of food for our whole party. These stores were equally divided by Carson himself; our own portion being the same as that of our men, and the whole would, with economy in using, furnish but three days'

SWIMMING THE RIVER.

scanty rations for each individual. Some of our men had lost their riding-saddles, and were fain to spread their blankets upon a mule's back, and jog along as they best might—a mode of travel which, when the animal's bones are highly developed, I take to be "bad at the best," for the rider. Others of the party had lost their clothing; and I am sorry to say that the number of pairs of "nether integuments" was two less than that of the people who ought to have worn them. But this was a trifle compared with our other difficulties, for there was nobody in those regions who knew enough of the fashions to criticise our dress; and as for ourselves we were in no mood to smile at our own strange costumes. Personally, I had been more lucky than the majority of my companions, having saved my precious suit of deer-skin, my rifle, and a few rounds of ammunition; but, alas! the waters of Grand River had swallowed up my note-book, my geological and botanical specimens, and many of my sketches, a most serious and vexatious loss, after the labor of collecting and preparing them.[3]

Two days' travel brought us to Green River, where we underwent much of the same difficulty in crossing which we had encountered in the passage of Grand River; but we had now learned wisdom from experience, and had, moreover, little left to lose.[4]

CHAPTER V

FROM THE GRAND RIVER TO TAOS

Short rations—Horse flesh—Failure of negotiations for a puppy—A deer hunt with Carson—Over the divide to Taos Valley—Indian sign—Mexican traders—Encounter with Indians—A tense situation—Carson's defiance —Retirement of the enemy—The first settlement— Arrival at Taos—Carson's wife.

THE dreaded "third day" which was to see us provisionless at length arrived, and, instead of breakfast, I tried to fill the "aching void" by drawing my belt a hole or two tighter; a great relief, as I can testify, for the cravings of an empty stomach.

As I rode along, reflecting, rather gloomily, I must confess, upon the position of our affairs, and considering where or in what form a supply might best be obtained, I discovered that the same feelings were occupying the minds of most of the party; and before we halted for the night it was moved, resolved, and finally determined, that the fattest of our way-worn steeds should be killed, dressed, and eaten. This idea furnished ample material for contemplation. Eat horse-meat! The very thought was revolting. I had heard of such a thing. Dana tells

some story of the kind, I believe; and I remember
the chorus of a nautical melody, deservedly popular
among seamen, which begins:

> "Old horse, old horse, what brought you here?
> From Saracen's Head to Portland pier,
> I've carted stone this many a year;
> Till killed by blows and sore abuse,
> They've salted me down for sailor's use."

And so on, through forty lines of doggerel. But then
the contemplation of horse-meat, as an edible, had
been with me but an abstract idea, which I had
never contemplated putting into practice. Now,
however, the thing was tangible. To eat, or not to
eat, became "the question," and, after due consideration, Hunger arguing the case on one side, with
strong Necessity for an advocate—and Fastidious-
ness taking the opposite, with Prejudice for her
backer, I came to the conclusion that I would not
and could not eat horseflesh. In accordance with this
valorous decision, although upon our arrival at
camp, a horse (lean, old, and decidedly tough) was
actually killed, cut up, and freely eaten of, I alone
stood aloof, and went supperless to bed. But it was
all in vain; for Starvation is a weighty reasoner, and
Hunger gained the day at last. I stood out like a
Trojan for eight-and-forty hours, and then "gave
in" with as good a grace as possible, and for more
than a week ate horseflesh regularly. Perhaps the

reader would like to know how it tasted. I can only
say that it was an old animal, a tough animal, and
a sore-backed animal—and, upon the whole—*I prefer
beef*.

During this period of scarcity, we met with several
parties of Indians; but found their condition little
better than our own; indeed, I believe that it would
have nauseated even a frequenter of a sixpenny
"restaurant," to have seen the horrible messes
which their women were concocting. But I had
got bravely over my squeamishness by this time, and
would have dined with a Mandarin, without ever
inquiring into the contents of the dishes. Really, I
blush to confess it—but I actually tried to buy a fat
puppy, which, truly and conscientiously, I intended
to have eaten. I enticed the brute (which, by the
way, was a short-haired animal, with a stumpy tail,
and a decidedly mangy look) into the lodge of its
owner, and then by means of signs, opened a negotiation for its purchase. I offered the extent of my
available capital—three cartridges and five brass
buttons. I said, "bow-wow," pointing first to the
dog, and then to my mouth, which already watered in
anticipation of the dainty; but though my proposi-
tion was comprehended, and the savage looked upon
the buttons with a longing eye, he seemed unwilling
to trade; and, finally, explained his reluctance, by
pointing with one hand to the puppy, while he gently

patted his capacious stomach with the other: thereby giving me to understand that the beast was intended for his own private eating. Finding that the dog was not to be obtained by fair means, and urged by necessity to secure him, at all hazards, I returned to camp, and dispatched "Juan" as a foraging party of one, to invade the enemy's camp and carry off the puppy, *"nolens, volens."* But he found the animal (who may have suspected something from the intentness with which I had regarded him) safely housed, and abandoned the enterprise in despair.

Upon reaching the borders of the Rocky Mountains, our situation, so far as food was concerned, became somewhat improved. We found this portion of the country to be by far the most pleasing and interesting which we had yet seen—every turning of the trail disclosing some new beauty of its grand and majestic scenery. Our course, except while crossing a dividing ridge, lay mostly along the mountain passes, where huge cliffs reared their rocky barriers, upon either hand crowned with various trees, the pine and a species of aspen being the most prominent. These valleys abounded in game, among which I noticed the black-tailed deer, elk, antelope, and the Rocky Mountain sheep or "big-horn," as they are sometimes called. This abundance, however, proved rather a matter of vexa-

ROCKY MOUNTAIN SCENERY.

tion than a real benefit; for the animals were so wild and unapproachable that our hunters were often disappointed in obtaining meat; so that but for the Indians, who were here better provided, we should have been obliged to return to the horseflesh.

I shall not soon forget accompanying Carson about this time, on one of our many excursions to procure venison. We had discovered a doe with her fawn in a little grassy nook, where the surrounding rocks would partially screen us from their view, while we crawled within gunshot. Dismounting with as little noise as possible, I remained stationary, holding our horses, while Kit endeavored to approach the unsuspecting deer. We were both somewhat nervous, for our supper and breakfast depended on our success; and we knew well from former experiences that if the doe heard but the crackling of a bush she would be off like the wind. Kit, therefore, advanced with somewhat more than ordinary care, using every caution which a hunter's education could suggest, and at length gained a point within rifle-shot of his prey. My nervousness was now at its height; why don't he fire? thought I. But Kit was cooler, and calculated more closely than myself. At last I saw him bring his rifle to his eye, at the same time showing himself sufficiently to attract the attention of the doe, who raised her head a little to get a look at the object of alarm, thus offering a better mark for his rifle; a moment more, and at the report of the piece, the doe made one convulsive bound, and then rolled upon the sward. To tie our horses, cut up the deer, and attach its quarters to our saddles was the work of twenty minutes more; and then remounting, we pursued our way, making quite a triumphal entry into camp, where Kit's good luck rejoiced the hearts and stomachs of every man in the party: it was really a great event to us in those days, and we had that night a right jolly time of it.

As the events here recorded took place when I was several years younger than I now am, I trust that the following incident will be regarded leniently by the readers of this off-hand, but strictly veracious, narrative. I relate it for the benefit of all romantic young ladies; and I may add, that although I consider the thing original in my own case, I have not the slightest objection to any young gentleman's doing likewise, if placed in a similar position.

To begin my story at the proper point, I must confess that in bidding farewell to the Atlantic coast, I left the object of a boyish flame behind me. A noble-hearted woman she was, with a very witching pair of eyes. (At least, I thought so then—but a plague upon such descriptions, say I. I never yet attempted to get through a lover's catalogue of lips and teeth, Grecian noses and ivory necks, and all that, without breaking down, so I will leave it to my lady readers to imagine all "my fancy painted her.") Suffice it to say, that she was a sensible woman withal, believing firmly in the old adage, "that a rolling stone gathered no moss"; and with such excellent principles it is hardly wonderful that she liked neither soldiers nor soldiering. But yet it was *one* of my first loves; a fancy of sweet sixteen; and campaigning had not altogether jolted her image out of my head. So one evening, as I stood upon a commanding height just above our camp, I thought of home and absent friends; until yielding to the duplex influences of a poetical temperament, and the solemn twilight hour, I fell into a train of romantic musings which ended in my cutting the name of my fair friend upon the barkless trunk of a gigantic pine, where it is doubtless legible at the present time, and may, for ought I know to the contrary, furnish some future traveler with a fair subject for wonderment and mystery.

The spot, moreover, had an interest about it beyond the mere fact of its lying amid the depths of a mighty wilderness, as it is said to be upon the line which divides the waters of this vast continent, those on the right hand flowing into the Gulf of Mexico, while those on the left mingle with the calmer waves of the Pacific. Were I in that region now, I think that I could almost find the identical tree, from the vicinity of a huge pair of antlers which I recollect to have seen lying near its base. If any man believes that the achievement was simply a "labor of love" unattended by any exertion, hardship, or danger on my part, I can only say that if he will stand upon the summit of an airy cliff, at the rather chilly hour of sunset, and cut three large capitals into the trunk of a very knotty pine with no better tools than a rusty jack-knife, I will give him a certificate for any amount of chivalry and devotion, and —call him a fool to boot.

From these rugged mountain paths we at length emerged, descending into the beautiful plains known as Taos Valley. Here we had scarcely gone a day's journey, before we discovered a great increase in the amount of "Indian sign," and also a change in its appearance, which, though hardly perceptible to an inexperienced eye, was too surely read by Carson's not to beget great uneasiness.

"Look here," said Kit, as he dismounted from his mule, and stooped to examine the trail. "The Indians have passed across our road since sun-up, and they are a war party too; no sign of lodge poles, and no colt tracks; they are no friends neither: here's a feather that some of them has dropped. We'll have trouble yet, if we don't keep a bright look-out."

Our camp that night was upon the borders of a stream which had been swollen by the melting of the

snows, until the neighboring prairies had been over-
flown to a considerable extent. This deposit of
water, now grown partially stagnant, had given birth
to myriads of musquitoes, who at evening arose like
a mighty cloud from their marshy beds to precipi-
tate themselves upon our devoted camp. Talk about
the plagues of Egypt! I will compromise for any
amount of frogs and locusts, or even take fleas, by
way of variety; but defend me from those winged
torments, called musquitoes. These fellows, too,
were of the regular gallinipper tribe, of which old
officers who have seen service in the everglades of
Florida tell such wondrous tales. To repulse this
army of invasion we made smokes, and hovered over
them until our eyes were literally "a fountain of
water"; but though whole battalions were suffo-
cated, and perished in the flames, millions rushed in
to fill their places and renew the fight. Our poor
mules, equally annoyed with ourselves, showed more
sagacity than I gave them credit for, by getting together in a body, and standing in pairs, side by
side, so that the tail of one was kept in motion
near the head of the other, thus establishing an association for mutual protection, which kept the insects
in some measure at a distance. But it certainly was
a ludicrous sight to watch the long-eared crowd
with their tails going like the sails of an assembly
of windmills, and to observe their look of patient

resignation when some musquito, more daring than his fellows, broke through their barrier, biting keenly in defiance of their precautions. Finding it impossible to remain by the camp fires, I at length rolled myself up in a Mexican blanket, covering my head so completely that I excluded not only the musquitoes but the air, and thus remained in a state of partial suffocation, listening to the shrill war song of our assailants, until the cooler winds of midnight forced them to leave the field, and take refuge in the oozy swamps.

We were up before the sun upon the following day, and continued on down the valley. Near noon Carson discovered a number of what appeared to be Indians some distance ahead, in a hollow, where a few stunted trees partially concealed them from our view. A little beyond their camp we perceived a large number of animals grazing, which betokened the presence of a party as large, or nearly as large, as our own. As these people were evidently unaware of our proximity, we called a halt, and after a moment's consultation, determined to make a charge, and as we seemed pretty equally matched in regard to numbers, to take, if necessary, the offensive line of conduct. With this view, we selected ten of our best men, and having arrayed our forces, came down, so far as determination was concerned, in very gallant style, each man with his rifle in his hand,

firmly resolved to "do or die." But, alas, for the
poetry of the affair, we could boast but little of the

"Pomp, pride, and circumstance of glorious war,"

either in our dress or accoutrements. "Falstaff's
ragged regiment," so often quoted as the *ne plus
ultra* of volunteerism, were regular troops when
compared with our dashing cavaliers. We looked
ragged enough and dirty enough in all conscience,
without any extra attempt at effect, but, as if to
complete the picture, the two unfortunate individuals who wanted "unmentionables" were front-rank
men, and your very humble servant, the author, had
a portion of an under-garment which shall be nameless tied round his head in lieu of a hat. Take us all
in all, we certainly did not neglect the advice of one
of Shakespeare's heroes, who bids his followers
"hang out their banners on the outer wall." The
mules, too—confound their stupidity!—ruined the
affair, so far as it might be considered in the light
of a secret expedition, by stretching out their heads,
protruding their long ears, and yelling most vocif-
erously. "Confound your stumbling body!" said
one old mountaineer to his steed (a wall-eyed
marcho), "maybe you'll have something to make a
noise for, when you get an Apache arrow slipped
into you." But our famous charge on mule-back
was brought to an abrupt and inglorious close upon

reaching the camp of our supposed enemies, by the
discovery that they were nothing more nor less than
Mexican traders, who had penetrated thus far into
the wilderness for the purpose of trafficking with the
Indians.

From these fellows we obtained some useful, but
not particularly encouraging, information, to the
effect that a party of mountaineers, larger than
our own, and better supplied with arms, had been
attacked by the Indians near the point at which we
expected to encamp that night, defeated, and de-
spoiled of their property. There was nothing before us, however, but to push ahead, and that evening
found few in our camp who cared to sleep soundly.
With a view to greater watchfulness, our guard was
doubled, the sentries crawling to and from their
posts; and all making as little disturbance as possible. The fires of an Indian camp—probably a part
of the same band who had defeated the mountaineers
—shone brightly from a hillside about half a mile
distant; and having nothing to cook, we deemed it
most prudent to extinguish our own, which had been
lighted to drive away the musquitoes. During the
night great uneasiness among the animals betokened
the presence or close vicinity of lurking Indians;
and Kit, whose long acquaintance with the savages
had taught him a perfect knowledge of their modes
of warfare, believing that they would attack us

about daybreak, determined to steal a march upon the enemy. In pursuance of this object, we saddled our beasts at midnight, and departed as noiselessly as possible, traveling by starlight until the first glimmer of the dawn, when we paused for a few moments to breathe our tired animals, and then continued on.

We had, upon leaving our last night's camp, nearly one hundred miles to travel before reaching the first settlements in New Mexico, the nearest place of safety; and it was now determined to make the distance without delay. Accordingly we pressed on as rapidly as the condition of our cattle would permit, stopping only to shift our saddles to one of the loose animals when those we rode showed signs of giving out. Late in the afternoon we had, by the free use of whip and spur, reached a point some eighteen miles distant from the first Mexican habitations.

I was just beginning to feel a little relieved from the anxious watchfulness of the last few days, and had even beguiled the weariness of the way by picturing to myself the glorious dinner I would order upon reaching Santa Fé, when Carson, who had been looking keenly ahead, interrupted my musings, by exclaiming: "Look at that Indian village; we have stumbled upon the rascals, after all!" It was but too true—a sudden turning of the trail had brought us full in view of nearly two hundred lodges, which were located upon a rising ground some half a mile distant to the right of our trail. At this particular point the valley grew narrower, and hemmed in as we were upon either hand by a chain of hills and mountains, we had no resource but to keep straight forward on our course, in the expectation that by keeping, as sailors say, "well under the land," we might possibly slip by unperceived. But our hope was a vain one; we had already been observed, and ere we had gone a hundred yards, a warrior came dashing out from their town, and, putting his horse to its speed, rode rapidly up to Carson and myself: he was a finely formed savage, mounted upon a noble horse, and his fresh paint and gaudy equipments looked anything but peaceful. This fellow continued his headlong career until almost at our side, and then, checking his steed so suddenly as to throw the animal back upon its haunches, he inquired for the "capitán" (a Spanish word generally used by the Indians to signify chief); in answer to which, I pointed first to Carson, and then to myself. Kit, who had been regarding him intently, but without speaking, now turned to me, and said: "I will speak to this warrior in Eutaw, and if he understands me it will prove that he belongs to a friendly tribe; but if he does not, we may know the contrary, and must do the best we can: but from his paint and manner I expect it will end in a fight anyway.''

Kit then turned to the Indian, who, to judge from his expression, was engaged in taking mental but highly satisfactory notes of our way-worn party with their insufficient arms and scanty equipments; and asked him in the Eutaw tongue, ''Who are you?'' The savage stared at us for a moment; and then, putting a finger into either ear, shook his head slowly from side to side. ''I knew it,'' said Kit; ''it is just as I thought, and we are in for it at last. Look here, Thomas!'' added he (calling to an old mountain man)—''get the mules together, and drive them up to that little patch of chaparral, while we follow with the Indian.'' Carson then requested me in a whisper to drop behind the savage (who appeared determined to accompany us), and be ready to shoot him at a minute's warning, if necessity required. Having taken up a position accordingly, I managed to cock my rifle, which I habitually carried upon the saddle, without exciting suspicion.

Kit rode ahead to superintend the movements of the party who, under the guidance of Thomas, had by this time got the pack and loose animals together, and were driving them toward a grove about two hundred yards further from the village. We had advanced thus but a short distance, when Carson (who from time to time had been glancing backward over his shoulder) reined in his mule until we again rode side-by-side. While stooping, as if to adjust his saddle, he said, in too low a tone to reach any ears but mine: "Look back, but express no surprise." I did so, and beheld a sight which, though highly picturesque, and furnishing a striking subject for a painting, was, under existing circumstances, rather calculated to destroy the equilibrium of the nerves. In short, I saw about a hundred and fifty warriors, finely mounted, and painted for war, with their long hair streaming in the wind, charging down upon us, shaking their lances and brandishing their spears as they came on.

By this time we had reached the timber, if a few stunted trees could be dignified with the name; and Kit, springing from his mule, called out to the men, "Now, boys, dismount, tie up your riding mules; those of you who have guns, get round the caballada, and look out for the Indians; and you who have none, get inside, and hold some of the animals. Take care, Thomas, and shoot down the mule with the mail bags on her pack, if they try to stampede the animals."

We had scarcely made these hurried preparations for the reception of such unwelcome visitors, before the whole horde were upon us, and had surrounded our position. For the next fifteen minutes a scene

of confusion and excitement ensued which baffles
all my powers of description. On the one hand the
Indians pressed closely in, yelling, aiming their
spears, and drawing their bows, while their chiefs,
conspicuous from their activity, dashed here and
there among the crowd, commanding and directing
their followers. On the other side, our little band,
with the exception of those who had lost their rifles
in Grand River, stood firmly round the caballada;
Carson, a few paces in advance, giving orders to his
men, and haranguing the Indians. His whole de-
meanor was now so entirely changed that he
looked like a different man; his eye fairly flashed,
and his rifle was grasped with all the energy of an
iron will.

"There," cried he, addressing the savages, "is
our line, cross it if you dare, and we begin to shoot.
You ask us to let you in, but you won't come unless
you ride over us. You say you are friends, but you
don't act like it. No, you don't deceive us so, we
know you too well; so stand back, or your lives are
in danger."

It was a bold thing in him to talk thus to these
blood-thirsty rascals; but a crisis had arrived in
which boldness alone could save us, and he knew
it. They had five men to our one; our ammunition
was reduced to three rounds per man, and resistance could have been but momentary; but among our

band the Indians must have recognized mountain men, who would have fought to the last, and they knew from sad experience that the trapper's rifle rarely missed its aim. Our animals, moreover, worn out as they were, would have been scarcely worth fighting for, and our scalps a dear bargain.

Our assailants were evidently undecided, and this indecision saved us; for just as they seemed preparing for open hostilities, as rifles were cocked and bows drawn, a runner, mounted upon a weary and foam-specked steed, came galloping in from the direction of the settlements, bringing information of evident importance. After a moment's consultation with this new arrival, the chief whistled shrilly, and the warriors fell back. Carson's quick eye had already detected their confusion, and turning his men, he called out, "Now, boys, we have a chance, jump into your saddles, get the loose animals before you, and then handle your rifles, and if these fellows interfere with us we'll make a running fight of it."

In an instant each man was in his saddle, and with the caballada in front we retired slowly; facing about from time to time, to observe the movements of our enemies, who followed on, but finally left us and disappeared in the direction of their village, leaving our people to pursue their way undisturbed. We rode hard, and about midnight reached the first

Mexican dwellings which we had seen since our departure from the Pacific coast. This town being nothing more than a collection of shepherds' huts, we did not enter, but made camp near it. Here also we learned the secret of our almost miraculous escape from the Indians, in the fact that a party of two hundred American volunteers were on their way to punish the perpetrators of the recent Indian outrages in that vicinity; this then was the intelligence which had so opportunely been brought by their runner, who must have discovered the horsemen while upon the march.[5]

It is almost needless to say that we slept the sleep of tired men that night. I for one did not awake with the dawn. Our tired animals too appeared to require some repose ere they renewed their labors; and it was therefore decided that we should take a holiday of rest before departing for Taos, now distant but one day's journey. I remember celebrating this occasion by visiting one of the Mexican huts, where I ordered the most magnificent dinner that the place afforded, eggs and goat's milk, at discretion—if discretion had anything to do with the terrible havoc we made among the eatables, a thing which on reflection appears to me more than doubtful.

Early upon the following day we resumed our march, and that evening terminated our journeyings for a season, by bringing us to the Mexican village of Taos, where I was hospitably entertained by Carson and his amiable wife, a Spanish lady, and a relative, I believe, of some former Governor of New Mexico.

And now, as our good parsons say, "a few words more and I have done," and I most sincerely hope that these farewell lines may not bring the sensation of weariness to the reader which I have sometimes felt upon hearing the foregoing announcement from the pulpit. What I have written is simply a plain, unvarnished statement of facts as they occurred. While I grant that the capital "I" has come in more frequently than I could have wished, I must disclaim all title to the hero-ship of my story. I was but a looker-on, "a chiel," who, though "takin' notes," did not then mean to "prent 'em."

Since writing a portion of the foregoing narrative, Mr. Christopher Carson has been nominated by our President to the Indian Agency of the Territory of New Mexico, a highly responsible office, requiring great tact, much common sense, and a fair amount of judgment. This excellent selection has been ratified and confirmed by the Senate, and I am free to say, that Kit Carson has no friend, among the many who claim that honor both east and west of the Rocky Mountains, who congratulates him more sincerely than myself. He is eminently fitted for the office; and all who know him will agree with me when I declare that I believe him to be

"An honest man, the noblest work of God."

INCIDENTS OF TRAVEL IN NEW MEXICO

CHAPTER VI

FROM TAOS TO SANTA FÉ

Description of Taos—Carson remains at Taos—A shot from
the brush—Wayside crosses—Camp at a village—
Father Ignatio—And his party—The Alcalde's hospitality—The wrong path—The wood cutters—Steering
gear for a burro—Arrival at Santa Fé.

As those who have followed me in my wanderings
through the wilds of the Rocky Mountains, and
amid the sands of the Great American Desert, may
not feel altogether uninterested in the continuation of my journey to the frontiers of Missouri, I
will resume the thread of my narrative from the
point where it was interrupted by our arrival at the
village of Taos,[6] in the Territory of New Mexico.

I have already stated that the way-worn condition of our animals, as well as the weariness of the
men, caused a day's delay at the rancho at which
we encamped before entering Taos, where we were
again detained for similar reasons from Saturday
until the Tuesday morning following. During our
sojourn there I visited most portions of the town,
which, beyond the fact of its having suffered in
former days from the chances of intestine warfare

147

or foreign invasion, has little to commend it to
the notice of the traveler. Its inhabitants exhibit
all the indolent, lounging characteristics of the lower
order of Mexicans, the utter want both of moral
and mental culture making itself everywhere apparent. These people, who know no higher duty,
and acknowledge no purer rule of conduct than a
blind compliance with the exactions of a corrupt
priesthood, regard honest labor as a burden, and
resort to it only when driven by their necessities.
Sleeping, smoking, and gambling consume the
greater portion of their day; while nightly fan-
dangos furnish fruitful occasions for murder, rob-
bery, and other acts of outrage. I speak of the
country as it impressed me at the period of my passage through it, some years ago, when these remarks were applicable to a large majority of its
male population. It is but just, however, to state,
that the women of New Mexico toil harder, and in
this respect are more perfect slaves to the tyranny
of their husbands, than any other females, if we
except the Indians, upon this continent. They are
literally "hewers of wood and drawers of water,"
but, unlike their cowardly and treacherous lords,
their hearts are ever open to the sufferings of the
unfortunate. Many have borne witness to the fact;
for the wounded mountaineer, the plundered trader,
and fettered prisoners dragged as a triumphal show

through their villages by men who never dared to
meet their captives upon equal terms in the field,
have experienced sympathy and obtained relief from
these dark-eyed daughters of New Mexico.

J C. FREMONT.

The houses of Taos, like those of Los Angeles in
California, are for the most part built of *adóbes,*
with walls of great thickness, the windows being
narrow, and strongly barred with iron rods, which,
while they afford a greater degree of security to the
residents in times of danger, give the place a gloomy,
prison-like appearance, which is far from agree-

able. In the arrangement of the interior of their
dwellings, as well as in the character of the furni-
ture which they contain, the New Mexicans differ
greatly from any of the Spanish race whom I have
hitherto seen. The sides of their rooms are provided
with huge rolls of *serapes* (a kind of coarse blanket, which forms one of their principal articles of
trade with the adjoining provinces, being largely
manufactured by the women of the country). These
rolls answer the double purposes of beds by night
and lounges by day. With the exception of these
changeable conveniences, the one apartment, which
serves as kitchen, parlor, and bedroom for a whole
family, boasts no other movables, unless, indeed,
some aristocratic *rico* indulges in the luxury of
a bench or table fashioned of native wood, and so
rudely carved and put together that it would have
done no great credit to the skill of our friend Robinson Crusoe, if found in his island habitation.

Both rich and poor, however, agree in appro-
priating one end of their dwellings to a sort of
family altar or chapel, where rude engravings of
saints, images intended to represent the Saviour, or
"La Madre de Diòs," sacred relics, and consecrated
rosaries, are displayed around a huge crucifix, which
occupies the centre of the wall on that side of the
apartment. These images, particularly upon high
fiestas and holidays, are decked out by the fe-

males of the family with all sorts of tawdry ornaments; and on such occasions it is by no means uncommon to see a doll representing the Virgin Mary arrayed in a muslin frock, trimmed with artificial roses, and festooned with ribbons of the gayest hues. Here and there are oil paintings; a worse copy of a bad picture, or, it may be, a veritable "Old Master," occupies the post of honor, and portrays saints, angels, and demons in every possible and impossible attitude, and engaged in every improbable avocation. As an instance of the singularity of these productions, I need only give an example of one of the ludicrous modes of depicting Scripture history which came under my own observation.

In the *casa* of a New Mexican *rico* stands, or rather hangs, a picture which I was requested by its owner to examine. He remarked that it was held to be uncommonly handsome, and valuable withal. After some little difficulty, I managed to penetrate the veil of dust, varnish, and asphaltum with which time and the picture cleaners had kindly shrouded it, and was rewarded for my trouble by the discovery that the artist (whose ideas upon perspective seemed somewhat *celestial*) had chosen for his subject the sacrifice of Isaac. Abraham—who stands upward of six feet—in a yellow uniform coat and blue striped pantaloons, with cavalry boots, spurs, and mustaches to match—is about putting an end to Isaac (whose dress, with the exception of the mustaches, is got up in nearly the same military style as that of the patriarch) by blowing out his brains with an old-fashioned blunderbuss, the muzzle of which is close to Isaac's right ear. The angel, however, has arrived just in the very nick of time; for as Abraham, with averted head, is pulling trigger, the celestial visitor discharges a torrent of water from a huge squirt directly into the priming of the gun, thereby saving the brains of the intended victim. As regards the coloring of this precious "work of art," I will only observe that it would probably, with a little smoking, bring a high price in the New York market as a most undoubted "original."

The concluding paragraphs of my Rocky Mountain narrative chronicled the fact that my friend Carson had a wife who was then residing in Taos. Now it was evident that Kit felt disposed to linger by his own fireside to the last moment which duty would permit; and when we remember the long and weary days of peril and fatigue which our adventurous mountaineer must necessarily undergo before revisiting his home, few of our lady readers will wonder at the wish, however strange it may appear to those unfortunate Benedicts who have found the silken chains of matrimony grow heavier in the wearing. To carry out his design, it was mutually agreed that I should depart for Santa Fé with the greater number of our men, and there await the arrival of Carson, who, with fresher animals, purposed accomplishing the distance—upward of seventy-five miles—in about one third of the time which would be consumed by our tired and foot-sore beasts in reaching their destination.

It was a pleasant morning in the month of June, at about ten o'clock—judging by the shadow of an old *adóbe* church, which serves as a sort of town clock or sun-dial to the denizens of Taos—when I bade Kit a final good-by, with a hearty shake of the hand, flung myself into the saddle, and turned the face of my "little gray," and mine own in consequence, toward that portion of our party who had already lessened the distance between themselves and "La Ciudád de Santa Fé" by a good Mexican league— which I take to be the longest in the world.

I had scarcely cleared the town by a couple of miles, when, while jogging soberly along with a greater feeling of security than I had hitherto experienced during my recent travel, I made my mule's laziness an excuse for relapsing into my old habit of day-dreaming; for the better enjoyment of which I got an easy position in the saddle, at the same time loosening the reins. It was not long—counting by minutes—before my sagacious "little gray" dis-

covered that she could loiter, for the time being, with
impunity. Having settled this fact to her own satisfaction, she next proceeded to slacken her gait from
a dead march to a shuffle, and finally halted outright, to devote herself to the more profitable dis-

ROAD SCENE.

cussion of the grasses fringing the roadside below,
while her master "chewed the cud of sweet or bitter
fancy" above. We might have passed a half hour in
this stationary way, the mule botanizing and I
ruminating, when, just as I had finished peopling
a little imaginary world of mine own, I found myself
"brought up all standing," nautically speaking, by
the sudden report of an *escopéta* fired by some un-

seen hand from the thicket-skirted bluff overhead; which, coupled with the sharp whiz of a ball within anything but a pleasant proximity to my right ear, astonished me not a little. But the *voyageur* through the wilds of the Far West soon learns to think and act promptly, and my two months upon the road had already given me some slight experience: so, without waiting for a verbal explanation, I sent a ball and half a dozen buckshot, as nearly as an off-hand aim would permit, to the probable whereabouts of my unknown antagonist; and then, finding myself contending single-handed with an ambushed enemy, and considering the chances of a fight under existing circumstances decidedly hazardous, I plied whip and spur with right good-will until my "little gray" brought me safely up to the rear-guard of our party. Upon relating my adventure, our mountaineers *allowed* that a greaser wanted to raise my *har;* which, being translated into plain English, signifies that I had that day served as a target for some prowling Mexican.

In traversing the old road between Taos and Santa Fé, the eye of the traveler is oftentimes arrested by rude wooden crosses half imbedded in stone-heaps. These crosses mark the spot where some one has been murdered by hostile Indians, or the equally formidable *ladrones*—as the banditti of Mexico are usually called. The stone-heaps which encircle the base of these rude structures are, as I am told, accumulated by a custom of the country which requires each Mexican who passes them to add a stone to the pile already gathered, and mutter a prayer for the repose of those who slumber so dreamlessly below. If the frequent recurrence of these sad memorials of crime be taken as a proof, the number of persons who die a violent death in New Mexico must be very great.

It was nearly sunset, when the close of our first day's travel brought us to the banks of a clear but rapid brook, which wound its way through the narrow street of a little Mexican village. Here we encamped; and while still engaged in removing the saddles from our weary beasts, we received a deputation of the inhabitants, who sent a *fair* representation, in the shape of some half a dozen *señoritas,* who brought eggs, goat's milk, and *tortillas*—the sum total of the products of the place. Each and all of these they were willing to dispose of to their *"amígos," Los Americanos,* for a pecuniary consideration. But, as their "American friends" were just then decidedly deficient in funds—five silver dollars being a large estimate of the amount of "circulating medium" in the hands of our party—and, moreover, as we confidently expected that the same state of things would continue until relieved by the pay-master, their traffic prospered poorly.

But our inability to trade seemed in no wise to lessen their sociability, for our visitors continued to come in until every man, woman, and child in the rancho had favored us with their company. Among others, the village priest figured most conspicuously, and, from his clerical dress, to say nothing of his ample rotundity of figure, attracted no small share of my attention. Were I to attempt a description of Father Ignatio, I should say that his style, though peculiar, was not unlike that of Saint Nicholas of Christmas holiday memory, for

"He had a broad chin, and a little round belly,
That shook when he laughed like a bowl full of jelly."

Indeed, I am inclined to suspect that the worthy priest was a man of the world, who loved better to gather life's roses than to encounter its thorns; preferring a good dinner and a long afternoon siesta, with other carnal enjoyments, or the performance of a penance or the keeping of a fast.

By nightfall our camp would have furnished a rich subject for Wouverman's pencil, as the wild-looking figures flitted to and fro; now strongly marked and standing out in bold relief against the ruddy glare of the fire-light, and then growing dim and shadowy as they retired into the gloom. We were a motley group withal—here a blanket-covered Mexican, with his gaudy *serape* and broad-brimmed *sombrèro,* and there a "Mountain man," who, with his patched and weather-stained hunting-shirt, long hair, and matted beard, looked quite as uncouth in our own fantastic garb; while at intervals amid the throng laughed a bevy of dark eyed *señoritas,* with flowing hair and coquettish scarlet petticoat, just long enough to display a taper foot and faultless ankle; who chatted and smoked their tiny *cigarritos* with a *sang-froid* and freedom from restraint which would have rivaled even the assurance of our fashionable belles. And now, though it be a digression, permit me to say that I like the style of these same daughters of New Mexico. There is little of the affected fine lady about them, it is true. They are nothing more or less than women; and, better still, woman as she comes from her Creator's hands, with eyes, teeth, hair, and figures—ay, and for that matter, *hearts* too, occasionally—founded upon the very best models—Dame Nature's own. In a word, they are women unstayed and unpadded, who have gained nothing from conventionalism, and have grown up to their full estate in blissful ignorance of a milliner's modes.

As I stood gazing upon the busy scene, thinking to myself that it would have seemed passing strange to some of my polished city friends, I was interrupted in my meditations by the fat fingers and unctuous voice of Father Ignatio, who tapped me upon the shoulder, at the same time whispering an invitation to drink a quiet glass of *aguardiénte* with him at his own particular sanctum, which stood, as its jovial occupant kindly observed me, at no great distance from our camp, near the end of the *cálle*.

I have hinted that the Friar was a "jolly dog." I will now go farther, and declare that his notion of a supper—a supper for two—was, to a man who had spent twelve hours in the saddle, by no means a bad one. True, we lacked deviled turkey and oysters; but the chocolate, and the omelette, and a "hotch-potch," savoring strongly of red peppers —prepared as my reverend host assured me, with an indescribable roll of his eye, by one of the prettiest *niñas* in the village—proved rather appetizing; nor was this by any means the ultimatum of the feast; for, with a sly glance from the window to discover if any prying loiterer was near—not (as the good father explained to me) "for fear of scandal; for a Mexican priest—*grácias a Diòs*"—(here the old sinner smacked his lips) "did pretty much as he pleased"; but lest some thirsty neighbor should drop in to share the liquor. My host unlocked a hidden closet in the wall, and brought forth a weighty flask, whose cob-webbed sides and well-sealed mouth gave fair promise of a good thing to come. The Padre's Bardolphian nose grew a shade rosier as he uncorked it; and his little black eyes fairly twinkled· as, with a laudable desire to prevent mistakes, he carried it to his lips.

"To your good health, my son; may you live a thousand years," said the Priest, as, after a preparatory dusting, he proceeded to test its contents.

I watched my reverend friend's movements with some degree of anxiety; for the receptacle, large as it was, was well tilted ere, with a long-drawn sigh and a look of fond regret, he lowered it to pass it to his guest.

And now, though the "Brick Lane Branch of the Grand Junction United Ebenezer Temperance Society" stood in the breach and forbade its utterance, I will say that that Friar was most assuredly a trump; for the flask, instead of containing the execrable *aguardiénte* of the country, as my first invitation had led me to suspect, was fragrant of as fine old Cognac as ever slumbered in the cellar of a gouty peer.

But as "enough is as good as a feast," and as I did not desire to follow too strictly the example of my reverend friend, who took his liquor in its primitive state, I poured a portion into a little tin "conveniency" which usually accompanied me upon my travels, and having added an equal quantity of a weaker beverage, drank, with all the ceremony which the gravity of our acquaintanceship demanded, to his Church, and its worthy representative. The ice being now fairly broken, the Friar came out gloriously, and told more good stories than my limited stock of Spanish would enable me to appreciate.

I have a recollection of assisting him some time after midnight in the performance of *La Ponchada,* the national air of Mexico, when, being a firm believer in the virtues of temperance and sobriety, and finding that my new friend was in a fair way to make a night of it, I rose, and plead my long day's march as an apology for so *early* a leave-taking—to the necessity of which the Padre most reluctantly assented, at the same time proffering his services to see me *safe home* (he had drunk thrice to my once), an offer which the unsteadiness of his legs might possibly have interfered with his fulfilling.

Had the Padre been wise, he would most certainly have followed my discreet example. But, so far from seeking repose, I caught, as I walked down to my camp, a glimpse of the reverend man, as he passed between the window and the light, with the bottle clasped lovingly in one hand, while the other kept time to the chorus of a melody which, so far as I could judge, savored more of punch than prelacy.

I must not forget to remark that the Padre's assistant (a little dried-up Mexican, the very antipodes of the priest) said something in the morning of a sound like that of a person dancing in the Father's room near daybreak. But this latter clause

must have been a scandal. At all events, his reverence professed himself unable to account for it,
unless, indeed, it might have been "a deception of

FATHER IGNATIO MOVED BY THE SPIRIT.

the author of all evil, who was ever on the watch to
take advantage, by interrupting the devotions of a
Christian like himself." I give the Priest's explanation in his own words; and for mine own opinion in
the matter, I can only say that I should be sorry to
differ with him in a thing of such trivial importance.

We were up betimes upon the ensuing day; but as I felt, after my vestry supper, by no means anxious to hasten our departure, it was fully ten o'clock ere we had repacked our mules and were once more ready for the road.

The bill of fare at breakfast was—thanks to the kindness of my reverend friend, the Padre, who came down to share it—considerably improved by the addition of some of the odds and ends of our last night's entertainment, to say nothing of half a gallon of goat's milk, and a couple of dozen of new-laid eggs, sent in by "particular request." And then, for pleasant company and instructive conversation to season it, I will back the jovial Friar (who looked as rosy and good-humored as if there were no such sins as old brandy and midnight revels in his decalogue) against any six-bottle parson in all Christendom, the English fox-hunting districts to the contrary notwithstanding. Long life, say I, to jolly Father Ignatio, wherever he may be.

But everything comes to an end at last in this sublunary sphere, and so did our breakfast, and with it my acquaintance with the Priest, who showered upon me every blessing of the Church as he stood by the wayside upon that memorable morning, with his bald pate shining pleasantly, like a mirror in the sun, waving his clerical *sombrèro* in the air, and shouting lustily after me until a sudden turning of the road hid our party from his view, and separated us forever.

Our journey for the day was marked by no particular incident, except that many of our mules showed symptoms of giving out; and even my indefatigable little gray, who had borne up amid all the privations of hard travel and short rations, threatened momentarily to drop down upon the road. But as we expected to reach Santa Fé upon the evening of the morrow we felt anything but despondent; and good stories, sly jokes, and pleasant allusions to our adventures by the way seemed the occupation of all.

Having completed our allotted distance, we encamped for the night at a rancho where a Mexican "Alcalde"—a very different sort of person from my friend the Priest—gave me a crusty invitation to supper, and nearly compassed the destruction of my digestive organs through the medium of over-done eggs and raw *aguardiénte*. I was the gainer, however, by his surliness, for it induced me to make a virtue of necessity, and retire at a seasonable hour. As I pronounced a benediction upon the servant of the Church, so will I record my malediction against the representative of the civil authority. That he may fall a victim to the miseries of his own society is the very worst evil which I could wish *Señor Alcalde Don Antonio Guerrara.*

Our start upon the third, and, we hoped, final day's travel between Taos and Santa Fé, was an early one. It was just sunrise by the luminary in question; not to mention an authority which, as threatening clouds were darkening the eastern horizon, might have been considered an equally reliable sign—I refer to the Alcalde's chicken-yard, a preserve well stocked with fowls, as I am inclined to suspect my unscrupulous follower Juan had ascertained during the night, or else whence came the raw material for the stew on which we breakfasted? Perchance it was an inquiry after one of his missing family that induced an elderly rooster, of corpulent dimensions and pompously martial air, to assume so elevated a position upon the posts of the *corrál*, and vociferate his peculiar reveillé so noisily, as our party filed into the main road. Let me advise the reader, if he should ever become a traveler in the provinces of Mexico, to instruct his servant in the art of foraging; for if he prove an adept, it shall be well for his master, who might otherwise go supperless to bed. To do my "treasure" justice, he was no fool, at least in that respect.

By noon we had reached a Mexican village, where, as Little Gray, my "ultimatum" in the way of transportation, was now upon her last legs, being scarcely able to carry herself, to say nothing of a rider, I concluded to tarry and dine, intending to push on

and overtake the party, or, at all events, reach Santa
Fé that night. I must confess that I was not a little
influenced in this determination by the bright eyes
of two new-made acquaintances—very pretty señoritas, who, in obedience to the orders of their papa
(Don Alphabet I shall call him, for his names seemed
legion), were then busily employed in cooking choice
specimens of the usual products of the country—
eggs, kid, and goat's milk. Apropos to which, it
appeared to me, in traversing New Mexico, that the
bill of fare in this primitive region would have
suited Alexander Selkirk admirably; for to that
hard-headed animal, the goat, the New Mexicans are
indebted not only for their food and bedding, but
occasionally for the very raiment which they wear.
Having finished my repast, which I took sitting *à
la Turqué,* using my hunting-knife and those yet
earlier inventions, the fingers, as a substitute for
the ordinary table implements, I lit a cigar, the sole
survivor of a treasured few; and with the aid of a
huge roll of *serapes* by way of a lounge, and the
Don's amiable daughters for society, I smoked and
complimented the young ladies in bad Spanish, thus
passing the time until *siésta* in a highly satisfactory
manner. This same *siésta*—which, by-the-way,
means in plain English an afternoon nap—was a
luxury which I had been wise to have omitted; for
I slumbered so soundly that it was not until the

lengthening shadows betokened the sinking of the
sun that I recollected the weary leagues between
myself and Santa Fé yet to be accomplished. Then,
with somewhat of reluctance, I ordered out my mule,
who had been dining in the *corrál,* and now came
most unwillingly to the door. Upon offering money
in payment for the attention which I had received,
it was, much to my surprise, and for the first time
in my campaigning experience, declined by my host.
So I had no alternative but to make my *"adios,"*
adding a *"mille grácias"*—thousand thanks—as a
receipt in full.

Once more upon the road, I experienced so much
of that chilly uncomfortable feeling which is connected with a departure from pleasant quarters, and
the undertaking of a long and lonely ride, that I determined to shorten its duration, if it were possible,
and with this intention halted to consult a peasant
who was lazily working upon one of the numerous
irrigating ditches which are the inseparable assist-
ants of New Mexican agriculture. This fellow, upon
understanding that I was in haste, recommended *el
señor* to take a certain by-road, which he pointed
out, assuring me that it would be the nearest by
more than a league. It was in an evil hour that I
listened to his advice, and departed from the beaten
track to follow an almost unused bridle-path, which
the gathering shadows of evening rendered yet more

indistinct. But, buoyed up by hopeful anticipations of rest, and a gay time in Santa Fé, I kept jogging on while daylight and twilight, and the pale radiance of a cloudless moon worked their changes in the aspect of earth and sky; changes which succeeded each other with a rapidity best accounted for by my own impatience and the solitary weariness of the way. By midnight I had become a firm believer in three conclusions: First, that I was lost. Secondly, that Little Gray and myself were exceedingly tired, and hungry withal. And thirdly, that the sooner we made camp the better. In accordance with this latter determination, I halted at the first pool of water, relieved my weary mule of her saddle and bridle, fastened one end of the *reata* round her neck, though there was no particular fear of her stampeding, as she was, in mountain parlance, "pretty much give out"; and then, with the rope twisted round my arm, for want of a better picket pin, I lay down to sleep, having my saddle for a pillow, and a sandy piece of soil—I always prefer that kind of ground—for a mattress. How gloriously I rested that night! You may talk of your sound sleepers on feather-beds in well-ceiled chambers, you city-bred people, who fancy you are enjoying robust health, and slumber like dormice! What do you know of "Nature's sweet restorer"? Why, I would not give one hour of that dreamless repose beneath the open sky, with the star-lit heavens above, and the pure night winds as they come surging over the dew-laden grasses—or, perchance, in lieu of these, a whisper of pattering leaves for a lullaby, and the dim forms of bending foliage, waving to and fro like gigantic plumes, until the whole grows shadowy and ghost-like as it fades with increasing drowsiness, for all your feverish visions, born of indigestion and an impure atmosphere.

The sun was at least an hour high ere his beams had gained sufficient power to recall me to the realities of this waking world, among the first of which I realized, as affecting myself personally, the facts that I had neither supped nor breakfasted, and, what was worse, stood little chance of doing either until my arrival at Santa Fé. Now, as one idea generally suggests another, this latter reflection brought me very naturally to the question, Where *was* Santa Fé? Was I in the right road or in the wrong? or—which seemed quite as likely—in no road at all? Should I retrace my steps, or continue on? All very proper queries, but somewhat difficult to answer, for the best of reasons—that I was very much in the dark myself. I had pondered these matters without arriving at any better result than a more intense degree of mystification, when, just as if to solve them all, down came a couple of Mexican woodcutters, with a little drove of *burros,* alias

jackasses, some of which were laden with wood to
an extent which left only their heads and tails visible, while others trotted loose, with but a saddle
upon their backs.

Having my mule all ready for a start, I mounted
and rode down to the pool, where the new-comers,
both bipeds and quadrupeds, were then watering.
Upon reaching the place, I first gave my mule a
drink, and then advanced to exchange the usual
good-morning, determined to obtain what information I wished, and, at the same time, impart as little
as I conveniently could to my new acquaintances.
But a Mexican is a shrewd talker, and in this particular instance they out-Yankee'd me completely;
for in ten minutes' time I had learned no more than
I had guessed at first—that they were wood-cutters
going to Santa Fé with their cargo; while they had
discovered that I was an American—a stranger in a
strange country—and badly lost to boot. As these
people purposed taking a short cut, or what they
called a *camino cerca*—near road—though I
would have defied any one but themselves or an
Indian to follow it, I concluded to bear them company; the more so as the elder of the two was a
curiosity in his way, with a spice of humor in his
composition, which exhibited itself in the caustic
speeches which this dried up little anatomy jerked
out occasionally, generally concluding a remark by

the personal application of a pointed stick to the ribs of his donkey, which never failed to call forth an indignant remonstrance from the injured beast. As we journeyed on in great good fellowship, I tried to beguile the tediousness of the way, which was just then leading us through a most uninteresting region, by arguing the question of Roman Catholicism, and its influence upon the inhabitants of New Mexico. Upon this topic I found the old fellow excellently disposed to agree with me; for the money, "which, with the assistance of Saint Joseph, he expected to receive for his cargo, would, *Valga me Dios,* be all expended upon his return in the payment of a certain debt, due for religious services and indulgences which he had obtained from the village priest, who would most probably" (added my informant, with a terrible punch of his *burro's* back, who resented the blow instanter by kicking out with a vigor which nearly dislodged its rider) "spend it at the *Monte* bank, or lose it at the cockfights after mass on Sunday afternoon."

While traveling thus, I could not but fancy that a schoolboy fresh from the wonders of the "Arabian Nights" would have likened my companions to Ali Baba and his son, and myself, perchance, to the Captain of the Robbers. Even I, with no great exercise of my ideality, almost expected that some rock would appear before which we would stand and

cry "Open, Sesame!" But my recollections of
"Morgiana" and the "Forty Thieves" vanished
most suddenly as Little Gray, fairly "give out" at
last, came heavily down, almost pitching me over her
head in so doing. Upon removing the saddle, I discovered that, at the best, I could only hope she could
be driven along barebacked until we reached Santa
Fé; and as her carrying weight was a thing impossible, I was fain to charter a jackass (which, for a
consideration, Ali Baba—for so I shall call him—
made over to me for my sole use and benefit), by
renting him for the next fifteen miles. So, without
more ado, I shifted Gray's saddle to the *burro*,
an ill-tempered, obstinate little brute, who looked as
if I could have transported him with greater ease
than he could have carried me. Having, by a great
reduction of the girths, got the saddle upon the
creature's back, where it appeared, by comparison,
large enough for an elephant, I then attempted to
bridle it—a proceeding which called forth, so far as
jackasses could exhibit it, an unqualified expression of disapprobation and astonishment from the
assembled drove, who brayed in concert; whereupon
the animal more particularly interested, as though
this flourish of trumpets had been intended as a signal, locked his jaws with a tenacity which defied my
utmost efforts to unclose them. Ali Baba, who had
been hitherto a quiet looker-on, now dismounted,

and explained to me that jackasses were an exception to all rules, being saddled, but not bridled.

"But how," queried I, "am I to guide him?"

"Nothing easier," was the reply. "You have only to use one of these"; here he exhibited a stick of hard wood some two feet in length, and sharply pointed at one end.

As I was still quite in the dark as to the manner of employing it, I took a few lessons in donkey-driving from Ali Baba, who gave me the following rules for my guidance; which I, alas! in my stupidity, reversed in their practical application, thereby getting into difficulties, as the sequel will show.

Firstly. I was to turn the donkey to the right by placing the stick before his left eye, the right optic being covered when he was required to go in the opposite direction. *Secondly.* To stop the animal, I was to wave the stick before both eyes; while to urge him forward, it was only necessary to punch him vigorously about the head and shoulders with the pointed end of my rod.

Determined to carry out my instructions to the letter, I got under way with the remaining quadrupeds, and Little Gray in front, while Ali Baba and his son brought up the rear of the party. For the first mile or two I got along remarkably well. But then my evil fortune took the ascendant; for, having had a slight misunderstanding with my jackass, who had thought fit to take advantage of my inexperience by doing pretty much as he pleased, I used my pointed stick to such good purpose, that the brute made off with a rapidity which fairly astonished me, and disgusted Ali Baba who, in the innocence of his heart, imagined that I desired to run away with his property. Having hailed me, under the influence of this supposition, in no very complimentary terms, which softened into a piteous entreaty as they discovered that I was increasing my speed, both father and son joined in the pursuit of what they appeared to consider a sort of American freebooter absconding with felonious intent. I was in a passion, of course. The idea was too preposterous—a lieutenant of infantry eloping with a jackass. But my mirth soon overcame my rage. It was a scene which would have excited the risibles of a Stoic. Just picture it to yourself. Fancy a young man some six feet high, dressed in buckskin, with long hair streaming in the wind, and mounted upon a stiff-necked and rebellious *burro*, who rushed insanely on, carrying his rider, *nolens volens,* into the thickest part of the pine woods fringing an abrupt hillside. Confound those same pines, say I. I have not yet forgotten how sturdily they stretched out their long, unbending arms, as if to compass the annihilation of my devoted brains—a catastrophe which the speed of my *burro* rendered not unlikely. But, with all these drawbacks, laugh I must, and laugh I did; for in my rear thundered Ali Baba and the jackasses, with Little Gray in their wake, whose familiar face was stuck knowingly out, with an expression which seemed to say, "Go it, master; this reminds us of our old times in the Indian country!"

Verily, it was a steeple chase, and over the roughest kind of a country at that—a race in which I should have come off winner or broken my neck, if it had not been rather abruptly terminated by my motive powers getting into a sand-heap, where I came to anchor very ingeniously by planting both feet, which my long legs and *burro's* short ones rendered an easy matter, in the sand. Here I was speedily overtaken by my pursuers, whose ardor, now that the chase was ended, seemed greatly cooled. Mutual explanations having satisfied all parties, except the *burros,* that it was entirely a mistake on their part, and ignorance of the art of jackass-driving on mine, we once more pursued our way; though I deemed it most prudent to keep within hailing distance of Ali Baba, whose experience might prove useful in case of another stampede.

It was not far from noon when, as we emerged from the pine-clad hills, I beheld for the first time our long-desired haven, "La Ciudád de Santa Fé." Impatient to get forward, I persuaded my com-

panions to urge on their *burros,* until, by the
vigorous exercise of their sharp sticks, they had
succeeded in punching them into a steady trot, which
soon brought us to the outskirts of the town.

Being not over anxious to exhibit myself upon
a Mexican jackass in the principal *plaza* of Santa
Fé, I halted at the Quarter-master's stables, where I
turned over my jackass, with a due consideration,
to Ali Baba, who made his *"à dios"* and departed.
My next proceeding was to rid myself of Little
Gray, who was, at my request, duly *installed* in the
Government stables, where both the accommodations
and the amount of forage on hand must have astonished her exceedingly. Nor was it without a sigh of
regret that I thus parted from the trusty companion
of so many weary miles of travel, who had carried
me safely from the distant plains of Los Angeles,
serving me faithfully amid mountain snows and
desert wastes; and—save in one solitary instance,
where she left me afoot among the California sand-
hills—conducting herself, for a mule, with undeviating docility. Poor Little Gray, I wonder upon
what rough road you finally laid down to die; for
"Uncle Sam" has, to his shame be it spoken, no retreat for broken-down animals, worn out in service
—a "Board of Survey" and a "public sale" being
their sole reward.

CHAPTER VII

AT SANTA FÉ

The United States Hotel—A gambling saloon—Lady Tules
—The priest—A custom of the country—Navajo Indians—Arrival of Carson—A change of plan—Departure of Carson.

BEING entirely unacquainted with the interior economy of the city I was about entering, I thought
proper to consult with one of the Quarter-master's
agents, whom I found lounging before the gate, as
to the whereabouts of the principal inn; which resulted in my receiving the information that the
"United States Hotel" upon the *plaza* provided
"chicken fixin's and corn doin's"—or, if a "stranger" wanted "Mex livin', *frijoles* and *tortillas* to
boot—in better style than any other establishment in
Santa Fé." Thanking him for his advice, and taking
the direction indicated, I walked slowly toward the
town, holding up my *serape* with one hand, while I
grasped my rifle in the other, cogitating, as I went, as
to the probability of the "United States" being willing to receive so ill-dressed a customer as myself.
Really it seemed more than doubtful, nor did a glance
at my habiliments tend to the relief of my appre-

hensions. I certainly cut anything but an insinuating
figure. My boots, between bakings in the sun and
drenchings in the rain, had changed their conditional
black to a positive brown. My leathern breeches, as
well as my fringed hunting-shirt, bore undeniable
traces of hard usage, to say nothing of sundry rents
which had been but indifferently remedied by Señor
Juan's attempts at needle-work—in a word, they
were greasy, blood-stained, and powder-soiled; and
as for my head-gear, why, the simple appellation of
a ''shocking bad hat'' would have been a complimentary epithet if applied to my private and personal *sombrèro*. All things considered, my *case*
looked badly. ''Well, never mind,'' was my mental
ejaculation; ''I'm tired and hungry—that's certain;
and if the proprietor of the United States don't
appreciate a gentleman in disguise, it's no fault of
mine. I'll state the case, argue the point, and enter
into all proper explanations. So here goes.''

Having come to this valorous determination to
face the enemy, I hitched up my leggins, and,
with a firm grip of my rifle, walked into the main
Plaza, where I halted before the door of the
''Hotel,'' a description of which may not be uninteresting.

As I recollect the ''United States Hotel'' in the
summer of 1848, it was a long, low *adobe* building,
with white-washed walls, narrow windows, and

earthen floors; its landlord and proprietor being a certain Mr. Ebenezer Spindle, a man whose long arms, long legs, huge nose, and cadaverous countenance had made him the wonder of his neighbors, who had seen fit to particularize him in familiar discourse as *"Long* Eben"—as they said, "for *short"* —a diminutive which I shall adopt in alluding to him.

"Long Eben" was a "Deöwn East" man originally—a fact which no one who had ever listened to his oracular remarks would be disposed to deny. He had migrated to the "Far West" when at the age of some five-and-twenty years—here he had gained

> "By what he called hook and crook, and
> What the moralists call over-reaching,
> A comfortable living";

or, in less poetic phrase, had ruled a country singing-school, edited a provincial newspaper, and occupied the stump political, where he made bad speeches for a candidate who was—not elected. How he got to Santa Fé, his most intimate friends had been unable to discover. There was a vague rumor in regard to certain "wild-cat" banking operations, wherein our long friend had been an unsuccessful speculator to an extent which rendered him anything but a favorite with the stockholders. There were even whispers of an indignant, but somewhat informal, meeting of the stockholders aforesaid; and a moonlight ride, which was somehow connected with a rail—I don't mean an iron one. But all this may have been a scandal. Suffice it to say, that he had "located" in Santa Fé, where he had chartered the "United States," and "allowed to tarry a spell if it should pay."

Upon entering the common room, I found "Long Eben" engaged in the concoction of a curious compound beverage, known among the initiated as a "gin cocktail"; which being duly discussed and paid for by the consumer, I beckoned to mine host, and calling him aside, asked—with some trepidation, I must confess, in my blandest tones—if he could accommodate me with board and a room during my stay in Santa Fé. After a little hesitation, and not more than fifty inquiries as to my birth, parentage, business, previous history, and future intentions, he "allowed they didn't calkerlate on havin' boarders to stop all night, but if I had a blanket he guessed they could manage to fix some kind of a shake down." So far, then, the thing was satisfactorily arranged; but now came the most important request of all, which, as the dinner-hour was at hand, I felt myself called upon to propound instanter. It was an awkward business, but with a preparatory hem to summon up my courage and decide upon the best

way of putting it. I blundered out the following
query:

Would it be considered decorous, or would I even
be permitted to appear among the guests at the
"table d'hôte" in my present attire; or, in other
words, was a greasy buckskin hunting-shirt, with
continuations to match, the style of dinner costume
then in vogue at Santa Fé? and could my host inform me of the whereabouts (I had just one *"réal"*
and two *"médios"*—total, five-and-twenty cents,
federal currency, in my pocket at the time) of the
United States Paymaster?—an all-important personage to a subaltern out of funds. It was an
anxious moment for me as I waited for his answer;
but my mind was speedily relieved by "Long
Eben's" ready rejoinder: "As fur what *yeöu* hev
got on, I calkerlate yeöur things is as good as mine,
and ef they warn't, I reckon yeöu could go to table
in—" (here he referred to the nether extremity of
a certain under-garment, which shall be nameless)
—"without any body's keäring ef yeöu did; and as
to the Paymaster, why, he lives jest reöund the
corner of the Plaza, and I'll send a young greaser [7]
with yeöu, after dinner, to show yeöu the way."

Here all further conversation was cut short by a
furious solo upon a bell, which, in the hands of the
"young Greaser" alluded to, announced to the world
in general, and the patrons of the "United States"

in particular, that "corn doins and chicken fixins were going, dog-cheap, at only fifty cents per head"; and I may remark that, had its tinklings been a special and direct call from the "Evil One" himself—had an earthquake capsized the "United States" and all therein—or had an elephant (always supposing he could have got under the door) walked in when least expected, I verily believe that each and all of these phenomena would have created less excitement than did the simple agitation of that brass dinner-bell. Through the front door at the back entrance, from rooms whose existence I had not even suspected, the famished bipeds came rushing in—the long and the short, the young and the old, all differing in their various externals, but all in pursuit of the same laudable desire to fill an "aching void" within. Finding that "self-preservation" was the order of the day, I pushed on with the throng, and secured a seat at a long and not very clean pine-table, whose wooden benches, earthenware plates, and ill-made cutlery might, to a less experienced man, have looked anything but inviting. But I was too fully impressed with the consciousness of long fasting to be overmindful of exteriors, and for the first ten minutes devoted my attention to the edibles before me with a zeal which must have persuaded "Long Eben," if he were a looker-on, that I should prove a most unprofitable lodger. Having satisfied my hunger, I yielded to the dictates of an awakened curiosity, and entered upon a series of mental note-takings in relation to the dress, conversation, and manners of my new messmates. It was, moreover, a favorable moment for my observations. The first heat of the onslaught was past. The clatter of knives, the rattle of plates, and the shouts of *"muchácho"* and *"hómbre,"* with which they demanded the services of the Mexican waiters, had given place to a comparative calm. The fat German opposite had paused in his feeding, and the nervous little Frenchman on my right no longer cursed the cookery. So far, however, as the jargon of tongues was concerned, the scene was a very Babel—French, English, German, and Spanish being all volubly employed to render the confusion more complete. We were certainly a mingling; and for costume, I felt almost at ease in regard to mine own as I criticised the dress of the people about me. There were men in jackets, and men in their shirt-sleeves—here a black coat, which would have been a credit to its wearer even on the right side proper (going down) of fashionable Broadway—and there a "hickory shirt," which had gathered the dust of five days' travel. Nor was our choice in occupation or position in life a limited one. There were old Santa Fé traders, who counted their gains by thousands, and whose signatures were good in St. Louis to almost

any amount; there were rough frontiersmen, who
boasted no "possibles" beyond the good rifle made
by "Jake Hawkins," which always "shot centre";
there were—but

> "I'll see no more!
> For fear, like Banquo's kings, they reach a score."

"Heöw are yeöu, stranger?" was my first saluta-
tion as I re-entered the bar-room, labeled "saloon,"
of mine inn, and on turning round to see who and
what manner of man he might be who took so tender
an interest in my personal welfare, I beheld a tall
Missourian, who, with the assistance of a chair and
three-legged stool, with the sight adjuncts of a small
carpet-bag and a large pine-table, was making himself as comfortable as the enormous length of his
legs would permit. "Heöw are yeöu, stranger?" he
repeated, as I continued to stare at him, still mentally wondering who this quaint specimen of humanity, with his wonderful legs, home-spun breeches,
and cow-hide boots could be. Having satisfied my
curiosity, I informed him that I was in my usual
health; upon receiving which gratifying intelligence
he arose, and, after stretching himself until I thought
of asking him to suspend so unnecessary an operation, finally remarked that "he allowed I had come
eöut thar to see the elephant," at the same time giving me an invitation to "take a turn round town."
Before starting, however, he sorely tested my friend-

ship by inviting me to join him in a "horn of Monongahele," as he was pleased to term some of the most
execrable "corn whisky" which it has ever been my
misfortune to taste. But I had sojourned in the Far
West too long not to know that a refusal to drink
would be considered anything but courteous to my
new acquaintance, or, as he himself would most
probably have expressed it, I should be open to the
charge of having made "a large hole in manners"
by so doing. Having, therefore, duly complied with
the stern requirements of frontier etiquette, we
sallied out together, my long companion taking
strides which would have done honor to "Jack the
Giant Killer's seven-league boots," thereby keeping
me at once in a dog-trot and a profuse perspiration.

Leaving the main Plaza, we traversed a compli-
cation of remarkably dirty streets until we halted
before a low *adóbe* house, built somewhat in the
form of the letter L, with a flat roof, and walls carefully whitewashed upon the outside—perchance as
a satirical commentary upon the purposes to which
it was devoted. But my guide was little given to
moralizing, or did not then care to indulge in it; for,
after beckoning with his hand, and muttering an
explanation to the effect that "they kept an elephant
in this establishment, and the *tallest* kind of an
animal at that," he made for the door, through which
he effected an entrance by stooping not more than

six inches. Following his lead, and keeping close to my conductor, I stepped into a room which, besides a couple of billiard-tables and a very mixed assemblage of the *"genus homo,"* contained a sufficiency of cut-glass decanters, not to mention a villainous smell of bad brandy, to inform me that it was the "bar"; but, as my companion had already paid his respects to the "Monongahele," he did not tarry, but glided through the throng, while I followed closely in his wake. A moment more, and we had entered another apartment, where the sounds and odors were, if possible, worse than those which we had encountered in the vestibule without. I now discovered that I had been introduced into the principal gambling saloon of the city. It was, as the exterior of the building had indicated, a long, low room, with narrow windows upon one side, which lighted it but dimly, and an earthen floor, which seemed perfectly impregnated with the expectorations of its tobacco-chewing frequenters. On either side of this apartment were ranged three tables for the convenience of the "banks" and their customers. These tables were strongly built of some hard wood, with a parapet upon the three sides most distant from the wall; partly, I presume, to prevent the money from rolling upon the ground, and partly, it may be, to put a stop to any undesirable scrutiny into the manipulations of the banker. Between the

GAMBLING SALOON IN SANTA FE.

wall and the tables were placed chairs for the convenience of the dealer, or dealers—for these gentry
usually hunt in couples; while upon the board was
displayed not only the *lure* in the shape of Mexican
dollars and Spanish doubloons, or "ounces," as
they are called in that region, but *a preventive* to
interference (or, as is sometimes the case, just com-
plaints of unfair dealings) in the shape of Bowie
knives, "Derringers," and "six-shooters," which
latter weapons lay prepared for instant use, being
loaded and capped so as to be ready to the hand.

The amount of capital invested in these operations was certainly much larger than I should have
supposed, several thousands of dollars being not unfrequently exhibited, with an assurance that even
larger sums would be forthcoming if the player
should desire it. The upper end of this "Pande-
monium" was occupied by a "roulette-table," the
proprietor of which kept crying out at intervals,
"Come up, gentlemen! Here's the game for your
money! Any time while the ball rolls! *Eagle* by
chance," and so on.

Finding that my new companion had by this time
forgotten me, and almost his own existence, in the
all-absorbing interests of the gambling-table, where,
if I might judge from his occasional exclamations of
"Wāl, neöw!" and "Wonder if that's *fār!*" he
seemed to be tempting Fortune with but indifferent

success. I made the acquaintance of a young volunteer officer, who was lounging about the room, and as both were but "lookers on in Venice," we joined company, and took notes, which at that time I had but little thought of printing.

It is a wise and truthful saying that "Death levels all things"; and if there be a parallel to that equality, which is only found in its perfection when we lie down "with kings and counselors of the earth," it is that born of the morally pestiferous miasmas of the gambling-table, where the one great passion absorbs all minor considerations—dignity, position, principle, nay, even honor itself, being forgotten for the chances of a card or the hazard of a die. Nor was it less so here, for amid the excited throng I noticed more than one woman—yes, even child— who was risking money upon the fluctuations of that truly Mexican mode of gambling, *"el monté."*

Among the females present, I remarked one, whose face—though she was by no means advanced in life —bore most unmistakably the impress of her fearful calling, being scarred and seamed, and rendered unwomanly by those painful lines which unbridled passions and midnight watching never fail to stamp upon the countenance of their votary. I afterward learned that this person was the most notorious, if not the most accomplished, gambler in New Mexico, where she had obtained by her unprecedented suc-

cesses a famous, or, rather, infamous reputation. As
her history is a peculiar one, I will give it in the
language of Gregg, who thus alludes to her in that
excellent work, *The Commerce of the Prairies.*

"The following will not only serve to show the
light in which gambling is held by all classes of
society, but to illustrate the purifying effects of
wealth upon character. Some twelve or fifteen years
ago, there lived, or, rather, roamed in Taos a certain female of very loose habits, known as *La Tules.*
Finding it difficult to obtain the means of subsistence in that district, she finally extended her wanderings to the capital. She there became a constant
attendant upon one of those pandemoniums where
the favorite game of *monté* was dealt *pro bono
publico.* Fortune at first did not seem inclined to
smile upon her efforts, and for some years she spent
her days in lowliness and misery. At last her luck
turned, as gamblers would say, and on one occasion
she left the bank with a spoil of several hundred dollars. This enabled her to open a bank of her own,
and, being favored with a continuous run of good
fortune, she gradually rose higher and higher in the
scale of affluence, until she found herself in possession of a very handsome fortune. In 1843, she sent
to the United States some ten thousand dollars to
be invested in goods. She still continues her favorite
'amusement,' being now considered the most expert

monté dealer in all Santa Fé. She is openly received
in the first circles of society. I doubt, in truth,
whether there is to be found in the city a lady of
more fashionable reputation than this same Tules,
now known as *Señora* Doña Gertrudes Barceló.''

The foregoing particulars were entirely confirmed
by statements made to me during my stay in Santa
Fé. This woman has since gone to render her final
account, and was, I am told, interred with all that
pomp and ceremony with which ill-gotten wealth
delights to gild its obsequies. Alms were given to
the poor, and masses performed for the repose of
a soul which could claim but *one* mediator between
itself and its Creator. When I saw her, she was
richly but tastelessly dressed—her fingers being
literally covered with rings, while her neck was
adorned with three heavy chains of gold, to the longest of which was attached a massive crucifix of the
same precious material.

Another ''noticeable'' amid this motley assemblage, who attracted no small share of my attention, was a Mexican priest, who, in the clerical garb
of his order, with cross and rosary most conspicuously displayed, was seated at one of the tables near
me, where he seemed completely engrossed by the
chances of his game, the fluctuations of which he
was marking by the utterance of oaths as shocking
and blasphemous as ever issued from human lips.

Unlike my jolly friar, Father Ignatio (whom may Bacchus defend), he sinned, not from carelessness, or out of a genial exuberance of animal spirits, but from the evil workings of the sin-blackened soul within. Yet this man was a minister at the altar, and a sworn protector of Christ's flock; who held, according to his creed, the power to absolve and to baptize, to shrive the dying and intercede for the dead; who would go from the curses of a *"hell"* to the house of the living God, and there stand in his sacerdotal robes and say unto his people, "Go in peace, thy sins are forgiven thee!"

As I was still following out the train of thought to which these matters had given rise, my meditations were interrupted by the sudden reappearance of my Missourian guide, who had lingered about Madame *Tules'* bank until he had staked and lost his last dollar. I shall not soon forget his woe-begone expression as he planted himself directly in front of me, elevating his tall form to its fullest altitude, while his right arm was gesticulating in the air. After looking full in my face for a moment, he addressed me in the following strain:

"I brought yeöu hiār, stranger, to see the elephant; but I kinder expect I've seen the critter wuss than yeöu hev. If yeöu'll take a fool's advice, yeöu'll leave hiār—sure as shooting and forgit the trail yeöu cum by. Darn the keärds!" he added, in a sudden burst of indignation; "I allers wus a fool, and cuss this Greaser swindle they call *Monté!* I *only* wish the man that invented it had had his head tuck off with a cross-cut saw just afore he thought of it—*wall, I do, hoss!*" Here he paused. I listened for something more, but he had "said his say," and, walking moodily through the crowd, which he elbowed with but scanty ceremony, he finally disappeared through the open doorway. The next time I saw him, he was seated upon the driver's box of a heavy mule-wagon, *en route* for Chihuahua, where, as he informed me, "he allowed to make a raise," being just then, "thanks to that cussed *Monté* woman, flat broke."

Upon regaining the, by comparison, purer air of the uncleansed alley-way without, I could scarcely avoid moralizing upon the scenes which I had so recently witnessed. Here were men, women, and children—the strong man, the mother, and the lisping child—all engaged in that most debasing of vices, gambling, an entire devotion to which is the besetting sin of the whole Mexican people. But yet these transgressors were not without an excuse. What better could you have expected from an ignorant, priest-ridden peasantry, when those whom they are taught to reverence and respect, and who should have been their prompters to better things, not only allow, but openly practice this and all other iniquities? If there be a curse (as who shall doubt?) pronounced against those who are instrumental in whelming a land in moral darkness, what must be the fate of those "blind leaders of the blind," the Roman Catholic priesthood of New Mexico?

On my way back to the "Hotel" I paid my respects to the paymaster, or, rather, to his clerk, from whom I received certain moneys due me from the United States for services rendered. Departing thence, I walked into a "store" upon the Plaza, where I purchased divers articles of clothing, with which, and a fit-out for my extremities in the shape of hat and boots, I so metamorphosed myself that a little Mexican, who had seen both my exit and entrance, grinned admiringly, which, coupled with the compliment of non-recognition paid me by "Long Eben" upon my return, was, all things considered, extremely flattering.

As it wanted still at least an hour to suppertime, that meal being served at the very primitive period of sunset, I once more sallied forth, leaving "Long Eben" lolling against his door, where he was busily engaged in completing what Dickens would have called "a magic circle of tobacco juice," to wander through the town.

Of *La Ciudád de Santa Fé*, as it existed in the summer of 1848, I can say little that is favorable; but as I am unwilling to pass judgment upon so limited an acquaintance, I prefer adopting a description of that city which I find recorded in the narrative of Gregg, to advancing my own hasty impressions. The more so, as I am satisfied that this description is not only the most correct, but the briefest which I have hitherto seen. He says, writing in 1844:

"Santa Fé, the capital of New Mexico, is the only town of any importance in the province. We sometimes find it written *Santa Fé de San Francisco* (Holy Faith of Saint Francis), the latter being the patron or tutelary saint. Like most of the towns in this section of country, it occupies the site of an ancient *pueblo,* or Indian village, whose race has been extinct for a great many years. Its situation is twelve or fifteen miles east of the Rio del Norte, at the western base of a snow-clad mountain, upon a beautiful stream of small mill-power size, which ripples down in icy cascades, and joins the river some twenty miles to the southwestward. The population of the city itself but little exceeds 3000; yet, including several surrounding villages, which are embraced in its corporate jurisdiction, it amounts to nearly 6000 souls. The latitude of Santa Fé, as determined by various observations, is 35° 41′ (though it is placed on most maps nearly a degree further north), and the longitude about 106° west from Greenwich. Its elevation above the ocean is nearly 7000 feet; that of the valley of Taos is, no doubt, over a mile and a half. The highest peak of the mountain (which is covered with perennial snow), some ten miles to the north-east of the capital, is reckoned about 5000 feet above the town. Those from Taos northward rise to a much greater elevation. The town is very irregularly laid out, and most of the streets are little better than common highways, traversing scattered settlements, which are interspersed with corn-fields, nearly sufficient to supply the inhabitants with grain. The only attempt at anything like architectural compactness and precision consists in four tiers of buildings, whose fronts are shaded with a fringe of *portales* or *corredores* of the rudest possible description. They stand around the public square, and comprise the *Palacio,* or Governor's House, the Custom-house, the Barracks (with which is connected the fearful *Calabozo*), the *Casa Consistorial* of the Alcaldes, the *Capilla de los Soldados,* or Military Chapel, besides several private residences, as well as most of the shops of the American traders.''

During my sojourn in Santa Fé I was struck with the very peculiar taste which the young ladies of that city display in their fondness for cosmetics. Indeed, when I first entered the town, it appeared to me that every woman under the age of five-and-thirty was afflicted with an inflammation of the face, which I had mentally concluded might be "catching"; in this belief I continued until my fears were relieved by the kindness of a friend, who elucidated the mystery by letting me into the secret. It seems that the *señoritas,* and, for that matter, *señoras* too, occasionally are in the habit of disfiguring themselves, by covering one or both cheeks with some kind of colored paste, which gives even to their village belles anything but an attractive appearance. This painting might, to the casual observer, seem intended as an ornament, got up in imitation of their Indian neighbors, or, it may be, of our own fashionable fair ones. But it is not so; for I am assured, by those whose opportunities of judging are undeniable, that it is put on as a preservative to the complexion. So that a New Mexican beauty is not only willing to forego the luxury of the bath, but even to appear hideous for a month at a time, for the sake of exhibiting a clean face and ruddy cheeks while gracing some grand *fandango* or *fiesta.*

There is yet another custom among these people which is well worth knowing, indeed, as applied to a "distinguished few," I would not altogether dislike its adoption into our own more civilized community. It is this: the New Mexicans greet a friend, not by compressing and then agitating his hand, but by putting an arm about his neck and literally embracing him—a nice, old-fashioned, patriarchal way.

This custom applies to all ages and both sexes; and really I agree with "Los Gringos" Wise, who informs us that "it is a real luxury to meet a pretty *señorita* after a short absence." But, like everything else, the thing has its drawbacks, and serious ones too. For instance, though it may be a very delightful thing to embrace, or be embraced by *Gabriélla* or *Martina,* or any other dark-eyed damsel of "sweet sixteen," it is anything but desirable to be obliged to extend the same courtesy to their brother *Juan,* or their *Padre Don José,* particularly if Messrs. *Juan* and *José* have dined upon a "hotch-potch" seasoned with garlic, which is but too often the case. As I said before, the custom is a good one, but in its practical application should be limited to one's young lady friends.

In repassing the *Plaza,* my attention was attracted by a group of Indians, whose dress and general appearance proved them to belong to some tribe which I had not hitherto seen. Upon making inquiry, I learned that they were Navajos, then detained as the somewhat unwilling pledges for the restoration of certain captives, and other property, stolen by their brethren from the good people of New Mexico and its vicinity. The accompanying "portrait" for the original of which I am indebted to the sketches of Mr. R. H. Kern, will give the reader some idea of their peculiar style of beauty.

It was at an early hour that my landlord exhibited the "shake-down" which had been prepared for me. I did not make the suggestion, but, if the truth be told, my first impression upon seeing it was, that a "shake-up" would do it no manner of harm. But a man who has lived out of doors for a month or two

HEAD OF NAVAJO INDIAN.

will scarcely grumble at a bed of any kind; so I said my "good-night" and tumbled in, but not to sleep; for either I was unused to being thus "cabined and confined," or it may be that the *chinches* (in plain English—bed-bugs), which swarm—as every New Mexican traveler is but too well aware—in this favored land, were too numerous for comfort. At all events, for some cause,

> "I turned, and turned, and turned again,
>   With an anxious brain,
>   And thoughts in a *train*
> Which did not run upon *sleepers.*"

Right glad was I to hail the first red gleam which came stealing in through the barred windows to announce the coming of the day; less pleased was I when, upon attempting to call a servant, I found that I had caught, thanks to sleeping in a draft, "a horrid cold," which would not permit of my speaking above a whisper. Pains in my limbs, and an aching head, were soon added to my catalogue of symptoms, and prudence confined me to the house for the two succeeding days, when Kit made his appearance—a very gleam of sunshine, if sunshine ever came in the garb of a travel-soiled mountaineer—to cheer my solitude, and inform me of his future plans, which were as follows:

He purposed obtaining fresher animals from the Quartermaster, reducing his party, and, by taking a short cut, go directly on to Fort Leavenworth—all of which was sad news to me; for I had already determined that, in case of his immediate departure, I should be obliged to prolong my stay in Santa Fé until I should be sufficiently recruited to continue my journey by a longer and less expeditious route. But, as better might not be, we parted—he to the free air and exciting travel of the Great Prairies, and I to mope within my solitary room, with the dusty Plaza and its low adobe walls to bound my prospect, and no better amusement than the study of character as I found it exhibited in the rougher specimens of humanity who frequented the inn.[8]

CHAPTER VIII

FROM SANTA FÉ TO THE MORA

Arrangements with a wagon train—Ruins at the Pecos—
The eternal fire—The Fourth of July—Whirlwinds
and mirages—Arrival at the Mora—A railroad to the
Pacific.

It was a joyful thing to me when that unwelcome
visitor, the "influenza," once more permitted me to
go abroad—a liberty which I was not slow to take
advantage of, by visiting one of the principal Santa
Fé traders, whose train was about returning to the
frontiers of Missouri. This gentleman received me
kindly, and on learning that I desired to accompany his party, offered me every facility for so doing.

As the train which I purposed traveling with was
already *en route,* having advanced as far as the
Mora, the usual starting point of the returning
caravans, where it was only awaiting the arrival
of wagons which had been left behind in Santa Fé for
repairs, and as these wagons were to leave town
early next day, I felt that I had no time to lose in
preparing for my new start. So, after divers con-
sultations with those versed in this, to me, novel
kind of travel, I provided myself with a good stout

mule, a buffalo horse, which I styled "Bucephalus" forthwith, and provisions for the trip in the shape of flour, bacon, hard bread, sugar, coffee, and so forth, each and all of which I found useful in their way.

It was not far from eight o'clock in the morning of a sultry July day that I mounted my "Bucephalus," who had been airing himself for the half hour previous in front of the hotel. As I had but two persons to say good-by to, my leave-taking was of the shortest. But in the case of Señor Juan, my old servant, whom I saw upon that sunshiny morning for the last time, I must confess that I experienced a greater feeling of regret than I had anticipated. He had, it is true, been with me but two calendar months, yet in that short period he had forded rivers, and traversed desert sands by my side; we had shivered in the same blast, burned beneath the same sun, and warmed ourselves by the same fire, until his image, uncouth and repulsive as it was, formed the back-ground of a thousand scenes not easily forgotten, and—hang the fellow!—made my voice a little husky as I gave him my hand for parting.

"Long Eben" was the last to say farewell, which he did in his own peculiar style, the "Deöwn East" drawl being still predominant—"Good-by, Mister; and ef yeöu meet eny body on the road that's beöund

for Santa Fé, yeöu may say that the United States
Hotel is a dreadful nice place to stop at, won't
yeöu?''

It was with no feeling of regret that I lost sight
of those piles of sun-dried brick which make up the
larger portion of *La Ciudád de Santa Fé.* I did not
like the place, I could scarcely have said why. It
may have bettered itself since, but it did not suit
me then. It is possible that the life of wild excitement which I had been leading during my Rocky
Mountain journeyings had unfitted me, in a measure,
for its every-day realities. Be this as it may, I had
had the blues, and, what is almost as bad, the influenza, in it; and once more upon my horse's back,
with my rifle in my hand, and the fresh breezes from
the broad prairies upon my cheek, I felt that I would
not have re-entered it for any consideration short
of a positive order from my commanding officer.

Our travel that day was marked by no particular
incident until our arrival at the Pecos, where we
encamped for the night. During our detention at
this point I examined some ruins in that vicinity,
which I found highly interesting, not only from their
antiquity, but from the historical events with which
they are connected. As I am already indebted to
Colonel Emory's report for the original sketches of
the ancient Aztec and Catholic church ruins represented in the cuts, and as I find the substance of

my own observations embodied in his journal, I shall take the liberty of quoting such facts as might prove explanatory or generally interesting. Under date of August 17th, 1846, he says:

"Pecos, once a fortified town, is built on a promontory or rock, somewhat in the shape of a foot. Here burned, until within seven years, the eternal fires of Montezuma; and the remains of the architecture exhibit, in a prominent manner, the engraftment of the Catholic Church upon the ancient religion of the country. At one end of the short spur forming the terminus of the promontory are the remains of the *estúfa,* with all its parts distinct; at the other are the remains of the Catholic church, both showing the distinctive marks and emblems of the two religions. The fires from the *estúfa* burned, and sent their incense through the same altars from which was preached the doctrine of Christ. Two religions, so utterly different in theory, were here, as in all Mexico, blended in harmonious practice until about a century since, when the town was sacked by a band of Indians. Amidst the havoc of plunder of the city, the faithful Indian managed to keep his fire burning in the *estúfa;* and it was continued till, a few years since, the tribe became almost extinct. Their devotions rapidly diminished their numbers, until they became so few as to be unable to keep their immense *estúfa* (forty feet in diameter) replenished, when they abandoned the place and joined a tribe of the original race over the mountains, about sixty miles to the southward. There, it is said, to this day they keep up their fire, which has never yet been extinguished. The labor, watchfulness, and exposure to heat consequent upon the practice of the faith, is fast reducing the remnant of the Montezuma race, and a few years will in all probability see the last of this interesting people. The accompanying sketches will give a much more accurate representation of these

RUINS OF THE CATHOLIC CHURCH AT PECOS.

ruins than any written description. The remains of the modern church, with its crosses, its cells, its dark, mysterious corners and niches, differ but little from those of the present day in New Mexico. The architecture of the Indian portion of the ruins presents peculiarities worthy of notice. Both are constructed of the same materials—the walls of sun-dried brick, and the rafters of well-hewn timber, which could never have been shaped by the miserable little axes now employed by the Mexicans, which resemble in shape and size the wedges used by our farmers for splitting rails.

The cornices and drops of the architrave in the modern church are elaborately carved with a knife.''

How graphic a picture does this description present of the sincere and disinterested devotion of these zealous but deluded worshipers—a delineation which, while it furnishes rich material for the exercise of a romantic imagination, affords much which should give rise to more serious reflections. On the one hand, it excites our ideality by producing to the mind's eye a representation of the scene. We behold the huge fires of the *estúfa;* we hear them roar and crackle as the silent watchers heap fresh fuel upon the blazing pile; we see the worn and wasted worshipers, whose hollow cheeks and attenuated limbs bear the impress of their painful and long-continued vigils. We can follow, in fancy, its devoted attendants, as year by year, and hour by hour, they fulfill their appointed tasks. We see them amid the summer's heat and in the winter's cold, shivering in the blast, or fainting beneath a sultry sun, as they go forth to procure the material with which to feed the flames. We can go with them during the long and dreary nights, when the exhausted Indian retires for a moment from the scene of his labors to cool his fevered brow and gaze upon those orbs, of whose mighty Creator he is so profoundly ignorant. We can be with him as he returns to renovate the dying flames, working patiently for naught, while the dark hours come and go, though the night-winds blow, and the pale moon shines steadily without; and even while the "gray dawn" is lighting up the misty hills, while sweet birds are warbling their matin songs, and all nature is rejoicing in the advent of the new-born day. Yet still he keeps his watch, forgetful of the world, with its myriad beauties, the creation of that master hand whose works are so full of strength, and dignity, and glorious perfection.

And this is Fancy's view; but there are deeper thoughts connected with the theme. Is there, in the self-sacrificing adoration of these benighted children of Montezuma, no reproof to the weak and vacillating spirit? No rebuke to the lukewarm ardor of those who profess, in this our enlightened age, to worship *one* God in spirit and in truth? Truly this is a subject upon which much could be written.

After our departure from the Pecos, we met with little in the way of incident or adventure which would be interesting if recorded here, save that some two days prior to our arrival at the Mora our teamsters celebrated the advent of the Fourth of July, and their own independence, by drinking an unlimited quantity of corn whisky, which ended in their getting most patriotically drunk; and calling into requisition the services of "Nigger Bill"—a little dried-up blackamoor, who on this occasion

danced "Juba," "by particular request," to the
sound of a violin played by an eccentric genius from
Kentucky, whose musical talents had already obtained for him the *soubriquet* of "Kentuck the
fiddler."

I derived, too, some satisfaction, while *en route,*
from a visit to a Mexican *rancho,* where, as I attempted to carry on a conversation in English, they
very naturally imagined that I understood no Spanish—a belief which led them into the double error
of supposing that I was just from "the States," and
might therefore be desirous of purchasing one of
those hairless, rat-tailed New Mexican curs, which
the Americans are in the habit of designating as
"cast-iron dogs"—an animal much valued in those
regions as a sort of four-legged warming-pan, to
which purpose these unlucky quadrupeds are frequently applied. The not very flattering conversation which ensued among its owners (who were
anxious to cheat me, if it were possible), as well as
their astonishment upon discovering that I had fully
appreciated their remarks, afforded me no little
amusement, which I finally enhanced by delivering
my opinion of themselves and their *costumbres.*

I was not sorry when we at length reached the
Mora, the literal meaning of which is "mulberry";
but, though that fruit is found in its vicinity, I am
inclined to believe, with Gregg, that it owes its ap-

pellation to some early settler of that name, from
the fact that the New Mexicans always calls it *Rio
de lo de Mora.* Here we found the train, or rather
trains—for they were three in number, though now
consolidated, for the greater security which an increase of numbers would afford—only waiting for
our arrival to make their final preparations and take
up their line of march.

I must not forget to remark that, during our short
detention here, I noticed some very peculiar effects
of *mirage,* or, as they are termed in prairie parlance, "false ponds"; as also the appearance of one
of those whirlwinds which are common not only to
the "great prairies," but to the sandy wastes of the
"California Basin." The accompanying wood-cuts
will give a far better idea of these phenomena than
any written description. So far as the whirlwind
is concerned, the explanation is a simple one, the
moving column being nothing more than a collection
of the particles of dried grasses or dust, which have
been taken up and carried forward by the eddying
currents of air, as I have seen water-spouts upon
that less substantial plain, the ocean. The *mirage*
is, however, not so easily accounted for. It has ever
attracted the attention, and excited much speculation, as well as no small difference of opinion, among
the *voyageurs* upon the great prairies. For myself,
I am inclined to concur in the opinion of a traveler,

who says: "The philosophy of these 'false ponds' seems generally not well understood. They háve usually been attributed to *refraction,* by which a section of the bordering sky would appear below the horizon. But there can be no doubt that they are the effect of *reflection* upon a gas emanating, perhaps, from the sun-scorched earth and vegetable matter. Or it may be that a surcharge of carbonic acid, precipitated upon the flats and sinks of these plains by the action of the sun, produces the effect. At least it appears of sufficient density, when viewed very obliquely, to reflect the objects beyond; and thus the opposite sky, being reflected in the *pond of gas,* gives the appearance of water. As a proof that it is the effect of reflection, I have often observed the distant trees and hilly protuberances which project above the horizon beyond distinctly inverted in the pond; whereas, were it the result of refraction, these would appear erect, only cast below the surface. Indeed, many are the singular atmospheric phenomena observable upon the plains, which would afford a field of interesting research for the curious natural philosopher."

As I have before stated, our sojourn at the Mora was a brief one.

And now, ere we bid each other, for the present, good-by, let me choose for my "finally" that much-vexed topic, *a rail-road to the Pacific. Can* it be

WHIRLWIND ON THE PRAIRIES.

built? will it *pay?* both simple and peculiarly American questions, which I shall answer in precisely the same manner that every practical man who has crossed the country would reply to a similar query. Let us look at the thing fairly; and, to do so, begin with the dark side of the picture:

Can it be built? The obstacles to its accomplishment are immense. Huge mountains rear their rugged bulwarks as if to bar its progress. Precipitous cliffs and deep *cañons* are in its path. Overcome these difficulties, and you have yet to struggle with the shifting sands and uninhabitable wastes of the Great Basin. Hostile Indians are to be subdued; wells dug, or water brought from long distances, to supply the hosts of laborers which so vast a work must necessarily employ. Such are a few of the popular arguments against its feasibility. But though they may and do exist, does it therefore follow that they are insurmountable? We shall hardly need workmen for the task, when every day is bringing to our shores crowds of able-bodied emigrants, whose strong arms are seeking employment within our borders. Have we not such men as Frémont and Beale, the former of whom, with the assistance of Senator Benton, has done more to bring this project into notice, and render it a possibility, than any other explorer? Have we not engineers of the highest order of talent? And are we not in this, the

nineteenth century, endowed with the enterprise to
begin, and the energy to carry out, this or any other
reasonable undertaking? In a word, do we lack

THE LIEUTENANT IN COSTUME.

that spirit, whose cry is *"Go ahead!"* I, for one,
should be sorry to believe that any American-born
man could be so far behind the age in which we live
as to acknowledge that an impossibility *can* exist

which Yankee ingenuity, and its servant, the steam-engine, are unable to triumph over. We may not live to witness its completion. It may even be deferred until the spring-time of our children's children; but the prophecy which hung upon my lips as our little band of way-worn *voyageurs* traversed with hasty steps the bases of those mighty *siérras,* will yet be fulfilled; for I am confident that the "iron horse" will one day thunder upon his rapid flight through these far solitudes, now so wild and tenantless. It is most undoubtedly the great task of our day and generation. Let us, then, snatch the honor of being its first projectors, ere "Young America" rises up to thrust aside the "Old Fogyism" of his fathers, and plant the corner-stone of this stupendous national work.

Will it pay? Need I answer the question. Look at the countless sails which are whitening the boisterous seas of the stormy Cape. Remember the multitudes who brave the pestilential miasmas of the Isthmus to reach the *El Dorado* of their hopes. Have the coasts of China and the Indian Seas no cargoes for our Atlantic ports? Has the great country across which the Pacific Rail-road would be a social, political, and Christian bond of union, no resources to be developed, no products to export?

Look at it in a military point of view. With such a facility, we could, in case of need, concentrate an ''organized militia''—that strongest safeguard of a free republic—upon the shores of either ocean. A few days' notice would place the ''bone and sinew'' of the West beside the hardy fishermen of our Atlantic seaboard. We should then be almost entirely secured against invasion from without, or dissension from within our territory. Such a work would do more to weaken sectional prejudice than the legislation of a century. Once more I repeat, *It will be done!*

IN THE BUFFALO COUNTRY

CHAPTER IX

FROM THE MORA TO THE PAWNEE FORK

The wagon train—The Great Prairies—Method of the march—Fight between Eutaws and Comanches—A ghastly target—To the top of Round Mound—The first buffalo hunt—A thunderstorm on the Cimarron—A stampede of buffaloes—A night march—The Arkansas crossing—Meeting with Aubry—Aubry's ride.

As Independence is the eastern, so may the Mora be considered the western prairie port of the great Santa Fé trail. It is here that the returning caravans make their final preparations for the trip, and catch their last glimpse of even Mexican civilization. The Mora is therefore, during the season of travel, a halting-place of no little importance, and presents at times, when visited by the busy traders, quite a lively appearance; indeed during the summer of 1848 there was scarcely a day which did not witness the arrival or departure from this camping-ground of a fleet of those prairie ships, the unwieldy Santa Fé wagons.[9]

I have stated in my "Incidents of Travel in New Mexico," of which this article is a continuation, that I had determined to accompany one of the numerous

parties then leaving for "the States." This caravan
—for it may well be called so—was a large one, consisting of three trains, numbering upward of one
hundred wagons in all. By thus uniting our people
obtained a more perfect assurance of journeying un-
molested through the hostile Indian range than if
we had pursued our course in smaller numbers; for
the Arabs of the plains—as the Comanches may not
improperly be styled—seldom lack caution.

Our party was made up of one hundred teamsters,
nearly all of whom were young Missourians. These,
with sundry traders, travelers, and Mexican herdsmen (whose duty it was to keep watch and ward over
an unruly drove of about five hundred loose cattle
which were to follow in our wake to the frontiers),
made up a force of one hundred and thirty men, the
majority of whom were sturdy, athletic fellows,
well armed with rifles, and though wanting discipline,
very fair material for a "free fight" with a barricade of wagons between themselves and their
enemies.

As it was at the Mora that I received my first impressions of the Great Prairies, it may not be im-
proper, before entering upon a narration of our adventures while in the "Buffalo Country," to attempt
a description of the peculiarities of this region which
I was so soon to journey through.

Mere words are inadequate to picture forth the

vast plains which are emphatically the "Great Prairies of the Far West." I am disposed to believe that the traveler feels this more fully in approaching them, as I did, from the westward than in the easier transition which is experienced in journeying toward them from the alternate hills and dales of the Missourian frontier, where the eye having no standard for comparison becomes familiarized to their peculiar formation, from the almost insensible change in the nature of the ground. But here— where their western barriers, the Rocky Mountains, tower aloft like the gigantic coast of an inland sea; where majestic steeps, many of them snow-capped or robed in clouds, seem saying to the grassy waves which skirt their pine-clad bases, "So far shalt thou come, and at our feet shall thy green expanse be stayed"—it is here, I repeat, that the *voyageur* feels most fully that he is gazing upon an unfamiliar land, for the realization of which no previous experiences of travel could have prepared him.

Clothed in the verdant livery of spring, or decked in the more luxuriant robes of early summer, they present the appearance of a sea of grass and flowers, save where some stream, fed by the mountain snows, stretches across the landscape, marked by the trees which fringe its banks and rear their wall of foliage above the otherwise almost unbroken level. Nor does a comparison between the prairies and the ocean cease with the great extent of surface presented to the eye: motion seems added to increase the delusion; each passing breeze, as it sweeps over the long grasses, gives an undulation to its ridges which is enhanced and heightened by the rapid succession of light and gloom derived from the shadows of flying clouds.

> "The clouds
> Sweep over with their shadows, and beneath
> The surface rolls and fluctuates to the eye,
> Dark hollows seem to glide along, and chase
> The sunny rides."

Nor are these mighty wilds solitary or untenanted. The buffalo feed over them by thousands; the timid deer or graceful antelope meet the eye at every turn; and the Indian makes them not only his hunting-ground but too frequently the theatre of scenes and conflicts the particulars of which but seldom reach the ears of the dwellers in our Atlantic cities.

There is a wild excitement, too, connected with the everyday life of the trapper and hunter in this section of the country which is almost incredible. So intense is it, in fact, that more than one young man, whose talents and fortune would have fitted him for the occupancy of a brilliant position in the world of civilization, has turned his back upon society and its refinements to endure the oftentimes fearful hardships of this adventurous career.

THE PRAIRIE OCEAN.

It is necessary to add to the foregoing observations upon the country a few explanatory remarks, which will enable the reader to understand somewhat of the interior economy and government of a Santa Fé trader's camp, as well as to give him an insight into the general routine of our prairie life. I have said that our caravan consisted of three trains. Now though these trains were for the time being united as a matter of mutual accommodation, it did not by any means follow that they lost their individuality; on the contrary, each train was still a little world of its own, being regulated by its particular laws and ruled by its special "wagon-master." This wagon-master is an all-important personage, whose authority is little less than that of a captain's upon shipboard; with this exception, perhaps, that Missourian teamsters are wild boys and hardly so obedient as a disciplined "Jack tar." The wagon-master is therefore a great believer in the force of moral suasion, and seldom resorts to knock-down personal arguments unless under circumstances of a highly aggravated character. It is part of his manifold duties to ride from point to point (for they are invariably mounted) during the progress of the train, as his presence may be required, to fix the camping-grounds, give the signals for halts and departures, and superintend the issuing of provisions.

Our everyday mode of life upon the road was very much as follows: The camp was awakened at day-break; and breakfast being prepared and dispatched, the cry of "Catch up!" from the wagon-master's fire warned all hands to get ready for a start. Then ensues a scene of noise and confusion which baffles description—a contest between unruly oxen who won't be yoked, and their irritated drivers who are determined that they shall. At length all is ready; and at the command "Stretch out!" each wagon falls into its appointed place, and with a universal crack-ing of whips we begin our march.

The rate of travel is from two to three and a half miles an hour, and the distance driven varies, ac-cording to the proximity of water, from fifteen to forty miles per day. Having reached the camping-ground, the wagon-master decides upon the position of the "corral," which is immediately formed by driving the wagons into a circular or horse-shoe form, where the tongue of the leading wagon which enters in advance rests upon or near the inner hind-wheel of that which follows it, so that each wagon overlaps the other, and thus forms a continuous bar-ricade, with the exception of an opening some twenty-five feet in width, left vacant to enable the cattle-guard, in case of an alarm, to drive in their charge. With a view to such contingencies the ani-mals are usually herded in the vicinity of this avenue, which can be closed by means of wagon-chains coupled together and stretched across the entrance.

The unyoking completed, then begins the business of the camp. The cattle-guard is detailed and takes its post. The cooks of the various messes (which number about ten men in each, and take by turns the office of cook and purveyor-general to their fellows) are soon busily engaged in collecting wood, or, if in the buffalo range, the dried excrement of that animal for fuel; the fires are kindled, and ere long all hands devote themselves most assiduously to the bacon and hard bread. Now comes the fun and jollity of prairie life. The labors of the day are over, and a little "euchre" or "old sledge" amuse some, while others try hunting or fishing if there be facilities at hand; or, what is yet more fashionable, spread a blanket beneath the shadow of a wagon, and doze until the sinking of the sun. By nightfall you will find the men collected in little groups about their respective fires, where they crack their rough jokes and relate their personal adventures in the way of hair-breadth Indian encounters or unheard-of buffalo shooting, until the watchful stars, the silver time-piece of the prairies, have marked the midnight hour, and they drop off one by one to their beds, or rather blankets, beneath the open sky.

The first rays of a July morning sun had not yet gathered sufficient power to dispel the low-lying mists of the prairie when those magic words, "Catch up!" transformed our camp into a very Babel, which was only terminated as the cry of "All set!" announced our readiness to depart; and ere many minutes had elapsed the word was given to "Stretch out!" and our caravan unwound itself like a mighty serpent from its coils, and took the great Missouri trail, which lay before us like a faintly penciled line toward the hazy horizon.

"Off at last!" was my mental exclamation as I lifted myself into the saddle; and as if to echo my thought, I heard a sun-browned teamster near me say to his companion, "Well, old hoss, we're bound for the States, sure as shootin'; and I'll allow that there ain't a man in this crowd that's better pleased to see the last of the Greasers' way of living than myself."

From the Mora we journeyed on for several days, passing the camping-grounds of Santa Clara Spring, Ocate, Colorado, and Punta del Piedras (Point of Rocks), without meeting with any adventure or incident of unusual interest, save an occasional meeting with an incoming train, whose travel-soiled wagons bore traces of Indian favors in the way of shot and arrow rents, until our arrival at Rock Creek. While here encamped it was reported among our men that a conflict had just taken place between a band of Eutaw braves, who had left their mountain haunts for the purpose of hunting the buffalo upon the great prairies, and a war party of Comanches, whose commission is generally a roving one, their object being simply to commit the greatest amount of rascality in the shortest possible time.

As the story ran, it appears that the Eutaws had encamped for the night, leaving a large portion of their *caballada* grazing in the mouth of a cañon at a short distance from their fires, where their owners, secure in the watchfulness of those to whose care they had been confided, felt but little anxiety for their safety. Just as the moon was rising the Comanches, numbering only sixteen warriors and two squaws, entered the other extremity of the cañon, and upon observing the horses, determined to gratify their cupidity, even at the risk of a difficulty with the Eutaws, who, in high good-humor from the successful termination of their hunt, were at that moment quietly seated beside their fires, peaceably enjoying themselves in their own fashion; which, in the present instance, signified squatting upon their haunches before the blaze and discussing their tobacco in blessed unconsciousness of the proximity of their new neighbors, or the unfriendly visit which they were contemplating.

The night passed quietly away; the smokers finished their pipes, and then lay down to sleep as men slumber after a weary march. The fires smouldered and died out, until their whitening ashes looked like ghostly shrouds as they lay bleaching in the moonlight, and the warriors on guard grew drowsy in their fancied security; when, just as the first dull glimmer of the coming day betokened the presence of the dawn, one shrill, wild whoop aroused our Eutaws to a sense of their danger, and with this Comanche reveille yet ringing in their ears, they sprang to their feet to behold their *caballada* flying before their captors up the steep defiles of the cañon, from the farther extremity of which the Comanches doubtless intended to gain the open prairie beyond: an expectation which was never destined to be realized, for though an Indian may be taken by surprise, he is seldom wanting either in expedients or quickness; and our Eutaw friends had lived too long in a bad neighborhood, and, it may be, stampeded too many *caballadas* themselves to be easily astonished, or to hesitate long upon their proper course of action.

Fortunately for the Eutaws they had a few of their best horses yet remaining to them, being those which, having been "hobbled" beside the fires of their respective owners, had consequently escaped the notice of the stampeders. To cut their bonds and fling themselves upon their backs was the work of a moment; and ere the Comanches had gained the centre of the defile with their ill-gotten booty the enraged Eutaws had overtaken them and were in their midst. It was now a hand-to-hand encounter, no quarter being asked and none given. The Comanches did their best by throwing themselves upon the sides of their horses and practicing every artifice in which the art of Indian warfare is prolific; but though they battled desperately it was in vain, for the death-dealing arrows of their foes made fearful havoc, while their own random shots did no material harm. The contest was too unequal to be long sustained, and ere the morning mist had lifted itself from the broad expanse of the prairie, or the red sun struggled out from the eastern cloud-banks to light up this scene of savage strife, the victorious Eutaws were again reclining by their fires, where sixteen gory scalps, waving ghastly in the breeze from their lance heads, and two lamenting squaws, attested the prowess of the conquerors. Had these unlucky females been wise they would have unsexed themselves for the time, at least so far as to have held their tongues; but, sad to relate, their grief overcame their prudence, and induced them to "give their sorrow words" in open defiance of the expostulations of their captors, until at length an old chief seized a club and settled the matter by splitting the skulls of both.

When this story first reached us we were disposed to regard it as a somewhat more than doubtful legend; but the ensuing day was destined to prove its truth, for as we neared the place I rode forward in advance of the wagons, thus preceding their arrival by upward of a mile. Upon nearing the locality indicated I observed a flock of vultures, which hovered like ill-omened spirits above the spot, flapping their broad wings as they circled lazily in the polluted air. Guided by their flight, I put spurs to my horse and pressed onward until I halted amidst the very scene where the conflict had taken place.

As I mused and moralized my meditations were interrupted by the cracking of whips and the vociferations of impatient drivers which announced the arrival of our train; nor was it long after the corral had been formed before our excited teamsters, many of whom were young Missourians embarked for the first time upon a prairie trip, came running up, and expressed, in the opinion of our older frontiersmen, a great deal of unnecessary astonishment upon beholding the nearly fleshless skeletons which strewed the ravine. Among our drivers there were men of the true mountain stamp, who had traveled, and trapped, and "starved it" until their hearts had grown harder than their hands. Men who had been down to Chihuahua, and weren't skeared at a redskin dead or alive—no, they would *"go under"* if they were—old fellows who had roughed it until they made it a point to be surprised at nothing, so far as prairie life is concerned. These reprobates, after

a careful search through the ravine, found one of
the Comanche skulls which had been picked almost
clean by the vultures and wolves; and having fastened this ghastly mark upon the end of a wiping
stick, they put it up at sixty yards and commenced
trying their rifles at one of the eyes, or rather at the
hole where the eye ought to have been.

It was late in the morning of the ensuing day ere
our wagons "rolled out" from "Graveyard Corral,"
as some of the old stagers chose to designate our
halting-place, out of compliment to the unsuccessful
horse-stealers. While awaiting the signal for departure I spent a half hour in looking up the skeletons of the unlucky squaws whose song of lamen-
tation had been so abruptly terminated. After a
careful search I finally found their bones beside the
ash-heaps which marked the location of the Eutaws'
deserted fires.

The next point of interest after leaving the scene
of the Indian massacre was a hill—if an elevation of
upward of a thousand feet can be so modestly styled
—which rises abruptly from the surrounding plain
between Rock and Rabbit-ear creeks. This hill is
known as the "Round Mound"—a name derived
from its circular, cone-like top. It is visible in clear
weather from a distance of many miles; and as the
optical delusion occasioned by the extreme rarity of
the pure and transparent atmosphere of the Great

Prairies continually deceives the beholder into the belief that much lesser elevations are close at hand when they are in reality some miles distant, it is by no means an uncommon occurrence for parties of two or three to detach themselves from the passing caravans for the purpose of visiting this remarkable locality. I, for one, have a painfully distinct recollection of the weariness with which my friend Mr. Danvar and myself dismounted to stretch ourselves upon the greensward at its base, after accomplishing the five instead of three miles which we had fondly imagined to lie between us and the object of our curiosity. How very unwilling we felt to undertake the ascent of the steep which we had so imprudently declared should be scaled, even to its top, before our return! But it wouldn't do to "back out"; it wouldn't do to be laughed at; and it wouldn't do to waste any further time in the enjoyment of our luxurious repose. So with heavy hearts and weary legs we proceeded to fasten our horses, and then commenced the journey upward. And "such a gettin' up," or, to speak more strictly, such a falling down, I never hope to see again. Thrice we halted upon the way and voted Round Mound a humbug, and our self-imposed excursion a most intolerable bore. Then Danvar would insist upon stopping to give vent to strong expressions; and yet another delay was due to a slip, which destroyed my equanimity and carried away the seat of a pair of buckskin pantaloons at one and the same moment. But "perseverance overcomes all obstacles," and by dint of puffing, blowing, and mutual assistance, we gained our goal at last. But having once reached the summit, fatigue was all forgotten as the delighted eye took in the wide expanse; on every side, a vast extent, probably upward of one hundred miles of country, was presented to our view. If we had been disposed to linger at our resting-place below, we now felt strongly tempted to make a long stay upon the crest. The distant wagon-covers of the far-off train had dwindled into snowy specks upon a perfect sea of vegetation. The emerald hue of the verdure at our feet faded with increasing distance into bluer tints, which in their turn became gray and misty as they neared the hazy horizon.

As we still lingered, entranced by the grandeur of so novel a scene, I was but too harshly recalled to a sense of this world's stern realities by an exclamation from Danvar.

"Hang it, there go our animals, or a pair that look amazingly like them! The sooner we get down again the better. I would not lose my buffalo horse before we get to Lost Spring for Madam Tules' bank."

My friend was off in double-quick time, and as I felt a great degree of interest in "Bucephalus," in whose come-back-again qualities, in case of a stampede, I had not the slightest confidence, I followed suit with all possible speed.

Upon "comparing notes" at the bottom of the hill, where I found Danvar rubbing his shins and groaning dismally meanwhile, we made the pleasant discovery that our apprehensions had been realized, and that our horses, tired of waiting, had pulled up their picket pins and stampeded. Luckily for us they made their way back to the train.

Two or three days after our Round Mountain adventure I had my first experience in Buffalo-shooting. It was a sultry day—the very hottest which we had experienced since our departure from the Mora. Remember, too, that a hot day in this locality is no trifling affair; for the "Santa Fé Trail" can sometimes, in the absence of that grateful breeze which usually sweeps these plains with the regularity of the Pacific trades, produce a specimen of warm weather which would do no discredit to the equator itself. The heated air appeared everywhere rising from the burning ground—the very oxen seemed an exponent of the enervating weather, as they lolled out their froth-specked tongues and panted wearily as they stretched themselves upon the grass. We had been encamped a full hour, and were now in that lazy, slumbersome condition which seemed to fall upon our people as regularly as the afternoon set in.

I had ensconced myself under a wagon, where I had made up my mind to remain and "take it coolly" until sundown. But who shall declare what an hour may bring forth, or where is the future more uncertain than upon the great prairies? I, in the innocence of my heart, was planning a quiet nap and the peaceful enjoyment of a cigar, when the cry of "Buffalo! buffalo!" resounded through the camp, and all hands, or perhaps I should say the "youngsters," turned out accordingly.

Upon springing to my feet to take a first look at the mighty beasts of which I had heard so much, I found the "buffalo" had dwindled to one huge old bull, whose shaggy hair and flowing beard gave him quite a formidable appearance; but so far from showing any particular fearlessness, the old fellow was even then "humping himself" to get out of our vicinity. One glance at the flying beast was enough for my enthusiastic self. I took the "buffalo fever" at once in its severest form, had my gun ready in the twinkling of an eye, and in less time than it takes to write it had sallied forth; and too impatient to await the saddling of my horse, had started off on foot, quite regardless of the "old stagers," who gave vent to their feelings in a subdued but expressive smile as they beheld my hot pursuit. It was, as I have said, an intensely hot day, and I half believe that the rascally old bull was amusing himself at my expense, by enjoying my vexation as I hurried breathlessly after him through the coarse grasses of the prairie.

After running the buffalo for upward of two miles, in accomplishing which he had repeatedly allowed

THE FIRST BUFFALO.

me to get almost within gun-shot ere he would gallop teasingly away, I found myself, in sporting phrase, "very much done up," and was about to abandon the enterprise in despair, when, to my great joy, the old fellow crossed a ridge, which not only served to screen me from his sight, but even furnished a cover behind which I could advance unseen. Having got within killing distance—which I did by crawling upon my hands and knees to the summit of "the rise"—I lay concealed until the movements of the animal should expose the proper spot at which to aim; that is to say, low down and directly behind the fore-shoulder; for if hit elsewhere the buffalo, who is exceedingly tenacious of life, will generally manage to make his escape, even though his wounds should ultimately prove mortal. Upon the discharge of my musket the bull snorted and jumped aside, but otherwise seemed but little discomposed. I then reloaded, and with a more deliberate aim fired a second time, but apparently with no better success. Somewhat piqued by my previous failures, I rammed home a cartridge, and was advancing for a third time, when I observed the animal to be lying upon the ground, where he was tossing his head and tearing up the earth about him with his short but dangerous horns. Fully satisfied that he was now completely within my power—for I had been told that the buffalo, under such circumstances, never lies down unless he has received a fatal wound—and elated by the prospect of securing him, I was so imprudent as to show myself to the infuriated beast. A moment's reflection would have proved to me the danger of this act; but in the present instance the reflection was an after-thought, and came too late. For, as if my presence had inspired new vigor into his wounded frame, the huge creature sprang to his

feet, and with something between a groan and a deep
bellow, which to my excited ears sounded more like
the first puff of a high-pressure engine, came dashing madly toward the spot on which I stood. There
was no time to be lost. To retreat seemed impossible, and no shelter was at hand; so, with a hasty
determination to stand still in "my tracks," and
trust my safety to the chances of a final shot, I drew
up my piece, with an inward prayer to the old gun,
as I raised her to my shoulder, to "shoot *centre*
now or never." There was a flash, a thin wreath of
sulphurous smoke floated idly up on the summer air
as the report of my musket resounded along the
prairie.

I looked toward the buffalo. The huge beast hesi-
tated as though he had felt the ball; then bounded
forward, stumbled, advanced again; once more stag-
gered and once more recovered himself; and then,
just as I almost seemed to feel his hot breath upon
my cheek, the creature fell headlong and rolled heavily at my feet, while the life-blood, welling from his
wounds, ensanguined the grass on which he lay. As
I subsequently discovered, my shots had all taken
effect; and the last ball, to which I owed my safety,
had struck him behind the fore-shoulder and had
gone quartering back: thus ranging directly through
the vitals. With all these hurts it was wonderful
that the animal had not gone down at once.

If my first attempt to approach the wounded buffalo had been too hasty, my present advance was conducted with consummate care. Indeed, after the exhibition of temper with which I had already been favored, I really felt delicate about intruding myself upon so irritable a beast. I retired accordingly to the skeleton of a deceased specimen of the same species that lay conveniently near, and there held myself in readiness to take my departure at a moment's warning, while I amused myself by throwing every available bone—concluding with the skull—at the ponderous brute which I had brought down. Finding him unmoved by these insults I made bold to approach the body, and having satisfied myself by numerous tests that the "vital spark" was actually extinct, I took courage, drew forth my bowie-knife, and proceeded to butcher my first buffalo. To do all things properly and in order I rolled up my sleeves, and having determined to take off the hide, which, with its recent ball-holes, would be an undeniable proof of my prowess in the chase, commenced the work. After making the preparatory incisions in a scientific manner, I began to strip off the skin, and for a whole half hour labored vigorously at the task, pulling, slashing, and hacking, right and left, at the huge carcass, with an occasional comment, "not loud but deep," upon the toughness of the beast, until I blunted the knife, lost my temper, and finally sat down to relieve myself by anathematizing the whole affair.

My situation may be briefly summed up thus: It was a broiling day; the perspiration oozed freely from every pore; the camp was some two miles distant; and I, in melting mood, was stretched alongside the stiffening buffalo, which I had killed but was unable to cut up. In short, I was exactly in the position of the gentleman who won an elephant in a raffle: it was a large elephant, a fine elephant, and all things considered a very cheap elephant at the price; but for all that the lucky man didn't know what to do with him. So, finally, I determined that, as the hide was not to be got off, I would content myself with the tongue, which I hoped to get out of its head somehow in the course of an hour or two. Falling to work again, I ultimately succeeded in getting out the lingual member. To this trophy I added the tail, which I cut off as an additional evidence that I had positively slain a buffalo. Shall I tell the precise time that I took to boil that old bull's tongue to an edible state of tenderness, and how we at length concurred in the judgment of Nigger Bill, who gave it as his professional opinion "dat if Massa Leftenant boil dat tongue till de end ob de world de debble himself would nebber be able to eat him"; or shall I chronicle the sly allusions to the *tale* of the "Lieutenant's buffalo"? On the whole, I don't think that I shall.

As we neared the valley of the Cimarron we found the soil growing much more sandy—a circumstance which added greatly to the labors of our panting cattle, who were frequently halted to breathe as they pulled the huge wagons over the heavy roads which we were now traversing. Our supply of water, too, except when encamped at the Springs (of which Middle, Upper, and Cold Springs are the principal), was of the scantiest; for, although our trail lay close beside the Cimarron, the name of river can only be given to it during the dry season by courtesy, and not, if water be necessary to the existence of a river, as its due. Indeed the Cimarron, which takes its name from the great numbers of Rocky Mountain sheep, or "Big Horn," found about its head waters (*Cimarron* being the Mexican appellation for that animal), is, during the mid-summer heats, nothing more than a bed of sand, with an occasional pool or buffalo wallow; for that animal frequently spends the hottest portion of the day in these natural bath-tubs—a fact which adds nothing to the purity or sweetness of their waters, as our parched lips could but too often testify. Water of an inferior quality can, however, be generally procured by digging for it in the sand banks, where the river sometimes is. It was in traversing this, the most arid section of the

Santa Fé trail, that the early traders experienced their greatest difficulties.

It was in the vicinity of the Cimarron that I witnessed, for the first time, one of those terrific prairie thunder-storms which are nowhere more terrible than in this particular locality. We were encamped upon a dead level; for fifty miles on either side of our corral there was probably no elevation higher than our own wagon bodies: we had not even the satisfaction of knowing that a neighboring tree might attract the electric fluid more readily than ourselves; and in this exposed situation we bore the brunt of a battle between conflicting armies of opposing clouds, which, I verily believe, approached more closely to the earth than clouds ever did before or ever will again. Yet, after all, there was something glorious in their conflict. I have seen the war of elements upon the great deep, where the hoarse murmur of an angry sea was added to the storm; I have heard the thunder ring and crash among the defiles of a Rocky Mountain gorge; but never have I experienced so fully the sense of a *personal malevolence* (so to speak) in the gathering and onset of a tempest as I did in this instance.

The day had been an unusually sultry one; and knowing that I should be called at midnight to take my tour of camp-guard duty (a service from which not even the wagon-master himself was exempt), I had retired to my blanket at an early hour, and there slumbered deeply until a heavy hand upon my shoulder, and a hoarse voice in my ear, saying, "It's twelve o'clock, Sir!" recalled me to the realities of this everyday world. Now there is nothing particularly pleasant in being aroused at midnight, or in being requested at that "witching hour" to leave your blanket and your dreams, your bed of prairie grass and your castles in the air—and all for the delights of a two hours' watch, with, it may be, a reasonable prospect of playing target to some prowling Indian before you are relieved. But although these matters were something of an old story to myself, I felt on this occasion a sensation of discomfort and a vague apprehension, or what some people call a presentiment, of impending evil, which I was at a loss to account for, and equally unable to overcome. But the guard duty had to be done at all events; so, under the influence of this latter conclusion, I groped my way, rifle in hand, to the half-extinguished fire, beside which the companion of my watch was already standing. After some little conversation, he remarked:

"We are going to have a rough night of it, Lieutenant."

"Why so?" I asked.

"I have crossed these plains seven times," was the reply, "and never before have I felt the air so

STORM ON THE PLAINS.

hot and stifling. We shall see a prairie storm, and no common one at that, before our guard is ended.''

I had barely time to remark the almost suffocating closeness of the atmosphere when a low, muttering sound seemed to verify his words; while the plaintive moan of the fitful night-wind, as it swept gustily along, seemed more like the wail of some restless spirit than the sighing of a mid-summer's breeze. Half an hour might have passed away, when, as I stood leaning upon my rifle indulging in the sombre fancies suggested by the deepening gloom, I was startled by a sharp, sudden flash of the most vivid lightning I ever remember to have seen. For a moment our corrals and the surrounding prairie were brought out with a distinctness that rendered even the most minute objects clearly visible; and then, as they relapsed into a blackness which, by comparison, appeared even darker than before, one tremendous peal, the signal-gun of the advancing storm, rent the air, making the very earth tremble beneath the shock. This was succeeded by a brief interval of repose, whose silence seemed, if possible, more terrible than the previous uproar; and then the thunder burst forth with redoubled violence, not in that low, grumbling tone which we are wont to hear when it wakes the echoes of some far mountain side, but with a force and energy that made us fain to bow our heads and cower before the gale as if Azrael himself had ridden upon the blast. And thus for two mortal hours did the tempest rage and the wild wind continue to do its work; while the rain, accompanied by hail, came down in torrents, saturating the thirsty earth until even the parched prairie could contain no more, and its overflowing waters gathered in great pools upon our camping-ground, in which we, the soaked camp guard, having arrived at that highly satisfactory hydropathic state in which one can be no wetter, stood at length with a proud consciousness that the water, so far as ourselves personally were concerned, had done its worst.

But the incidents of this eventful night were not yet ended. Though the fury of the storm was past, we were destined to witness a new and scarcely less exciting spectacle. By the now increasing light I had observed my companion bending his ear toward the earth as though he had caught some sound which he wished to hear more perfectly; and ere the lips could form the words to put a question, my own ear remarked a faint continuous rumbling which, though hardly perceivable at first, grew more and more distinct as it came swelling up from the south-west. As it continued to increase I asked, "What can that mean? It is certainly not the storm, for that is breaking; besides, the noise is too continuous and evidently comes nearer."

"I know it is not the storm, for neither wind nor the muttering of distant thunder gives out a sound like that," was the quiet reply.

"You don't mean to say that it's the trampling of the horses of a band of Indians, do you? This is no time for even a Comanche to be abroad, and neither gunpowder nor bow-strings would do their work properly to-night."

"Never mind what it is, Lieutenant, we can do no manner of good here; and if it is what I think, a thousand men would no more stay their progress than one of Jake Hawkins's rifles could fail to shoot centre in a mountain man's hands."

By this time we had reached the mouth of the corral, where my companion examined the fastening of the chain which secured its entrance, muttering, as he did so, "It ain't no use; iron won't stop them if they head this way."

The tempest, as I have already remarked, had abated; and as if to light up the strange, and, withal, somewhat fearful sight which we were about to witness, the stars began to struggle out from the fast-dissolving cloud-banks. Glancing in the direction from whence the first alarm had come, I had no longer any need to ask its meaning; for I beheld, toward the south-west, a dark mass of living creatures advancing across the prairie with the rapidity of a horse at speed, but so compactly, and

with so uniform a movement, that but for the trampling of the myriads of hoofs, which seemed to
shake the very ground on which we stood, I should
hardly have supposed, by that uncertain light, that
a countless herd of buffalo were stampeding before
the storm; [10] but so it was, and fortunately for us
their leaders took a course which brought this tremendous drove within some ten or fifteen yards of
our encampment instead of dashing them against
our wagons. Had they done otherwise, the trepidation which our presence would have excited among
the foremost could have been of no avail, as the
weight of the frightened mass, who were pressing
close upon their rear, would inevitably have forced
them forward, and brought the herd, willing or unwilling, into contact with our corrals. For nearly
an hour the buffaloes continued to pass by. I have
no words to do justice to the scene. I must therefore leave it to the imagination of the reader to fill
up the details of so unusual a spectacle. Let him
fancy the uproar of their deep bellowings—the shock
of their heavy hoofs—the wild night—the recently
storm-swept prairie—the starlit sky, with its hurry-
ing clouds—and, lastly, the certainty of their doing
us a mischief should they change their course—and
I think that he will agree with me when I say that,
taking it all in all, the *romance* of the thing being
duly considered, I have but little liking for such

midnight cattle-shows, and should much prefer to take their singularity for granted than to witness it personally for the second time.

Between the Cimarron and the crossing of the Arkansas lies a long arid stretch or *jornada;* and as no water is to be found upon the trail, it becomes necessary to prepare the caravan previously to its setting out for encountering the difficulties of what, in prairie parlance, is usually termed a "water-scrape." With a view to such contingencies each wagon is, when properly equipped, provided with a five-gallon water-keg, which is, or ought to be, filled just before starting. In the present instance, as the pull would be a heavy one and the day was excessively hot, the wagon-masters determined to make the greater part of the distance by moonlight, or starlight if no moonshine could be had. We did not therefore leave camp until early in the afternoon, when, in compliance with the order to "stretch out," I once more mounted Bucephalus and jogged soberly along, meeting for days with no special incident.

The first rays of the morning sun were glittering upon the broad bosom of the shallow Arkansas as our leading wagons entered the stream. It was a pleasant sight to gaze upon withal, for here at last was something tangible. I stood at length upon the banks of a tributary to the "Great Father of

Waters''; and as the pleased eye beheld the gliding of its tide, I almost fancied myself in a civilized land, when—just my luck—down comes Bucephalus, who banishes my day-dreams with a vengeance by precipitating me neck and heels into the very waters which I had been so gladly contemplating. I had been brought down from my high horse in more respects than one, and gained the opposite bank in a very matter-of-fact mood, where, with teeth chattering my head, I straightway fell to moralizing upon the uncertainty of stumbling horses, and the vanity of building castles in the air.

It was therefore with no slight degree of gratification that I heard our ''wagon-master'' direct his teamster to ''drive up and corral''; which, being done, I managed to secure a blanket, and, having shrouded myself therein, notified ''Nigga Bill,'' our man of all work, that he would, at his own personal peril, permit any man to disturb my slumbers, unless, indeed, the Comanches should make an inroad into the camp, and not even then if he could help it. I am inclined to believe that my nap that morning would have astonished the ''Seven Sleepers'' had those worthy gentlemen been present and wakeful enough to have appreciated my performances. Be this as it may, I slept like a dormouse in winter-quarters until the full vigor of the mid-day sun convinced me that my covering was somewhat of the warmest; whereupon I went through the usual preparatory formula of yawnings, extension movements, and other matters of that sort, and then—awoke outright.

As I raised myself into a sitting posture upon my blanket my ear was attracted by a gradually increasing sound which soon resolved itself into the roll of an approaching train, and ere long the snowy tops of some sixty-odd heavy mule-wagons made their appearance above the ridge, through whose undulations lay the road which we had yet to travel.

Having halted their caravan, the strangers next proceeded to make camp in our vicinity: but as a meeting with a train had been an event of almost daily occurrence since our departure from the Mora, I felt no particular interest in regard to the newcomers until sometime after they had "corraled"; when one of our party, who had "been visiting," informed me that these wagons were, for the most part, owned by that singularly enterprising Santa Fé trader, Aubrey, who was then accompanying them.[11]

Now as "Little Aubrey" had become almost as familiar an appellation among Western men as a Jake Hawkins rifle, I determined to go over and pay my respects forthwith. So, after making a hasty toilet in true prairie style—which is much like that of a Newfoundland dog, by giving yourself a succession of shakes—I took my rifle (always a wise precaution upon the Plains) and started for the fires of our new neighbors. Upon reaching their corral I found Aubrey, with a few of his friends, seated upon the ground, where they were encircling a gaudy serape, which had been stretched out as a dining-table for the traders. Having been introduced to Aubrey, who invited me to join their party, and "take prairie fare, if I could eat fat cow," I made myself perfectly at home by sitting down forthwith and securing a fair share of "elbow-room," while black Juba, Aubrey's sable valet, supplied me with the instruments for the coming onslaught upon the cookery.

The dinner equipage was of the plainest, being nothing more than a three-legged iron pot, while to each guest was allotted a tin cup, a pewter soup-plate, and accessories to match. In this latter respect, however, the demand upon black Juba was slight, as most of the gentlemen brought their own tools with them. You may talk about your venison and your South Down mutton, but let me assure you that when our host's black boy opened that same three-legged iron pot, with a flourish which would have done honor to the best-drilled waiter of a fashionable hotel, I would not have exchanged the savory smell—to say nothing of the substance of that buffalo-stew—for your nick-nacks. In mountain parlance "Buffler meat ain't bad, 'specially fat cow, and hump-ribs at that—*well,* it ain't."

We cleared our dishes till black Jake fell into a profuse perspiration, and exhausted nature could achieve no more; and then sunk back upon our blankets to enjoy our brandy-and-water (for few men are teetotalers if they can help it when west of the Council Grove), and watch the airy smoke-wreaths as they went circling upward from some of the very best cigars which had crossed my lip since our departure from Los Angeles.

"Little Aubrey," like my friend Kit Carson—whose portrait, as he appeared when I knew him, is herewith given—is (alas that I should now say *was*) a man of medium stature and slender proportions, with keen eyes, iron nerve, great resolution, and indomitable perseverance. As a Western pioneer he has done much which would be well worthy of mention, but I shall relate but one of his adventurous feats—his astonishing ride from Santa Fé to Independence, in Missouri, a distance of 780 miles, which he accomplished during the early summer of 1848, in the incredibly short period of less than eight successive days. The circumstances are as follows:

Aubrey had come out, early in the spring of 1848, with a large amount of goods to Santa Fé. As the American troops were then in possession of the country, our merchants, relieved from the interfer-

Your sincere friend
C. Carson—

ence of those unscrupulous plunderers, the Mexican
custom-house officers, found increased competition
but greater facilities for their trade. Business was
therefore "looking up," and Aubrey found no difficulty in getting rid of his stock, at an advance which
netted him, as stated, over 100 per cent. upon his
original investment. Knowing the favorable state
of the market, and the description of merchandise
best suited to its wants, our trader determined to
attempt a hitherto unheard of enterprise, by making
a second trip to St. Louis, and bringing out another
stock before the cold weather should embarrass the
communication between Santa Fé and the Settlements. To accomplish this Aubrey allowed himself
but eight days to traverse the whole Santa Fé trail,
most of which is dangerous on account of Indians.
Having laid his plans and announced his scheme,
Aubrey then undertook to convince his unbelieving
friends, by offering to wager a considerable sum that
he would come in within his time. Now as a bet,
particularly with the "money up," seldom goes a
begging in New Mexico, it was not long ere some
confident individual expressed his willingness to
"size" Aubrey's "pile"; and as one wager begets
another, the subject became a fashionable point to
differ upon, and many were the boots, and numerous
the hats, to say nothing of the "tens" and "twen-
ties" which were hazarded upon Aubrey's "inten-

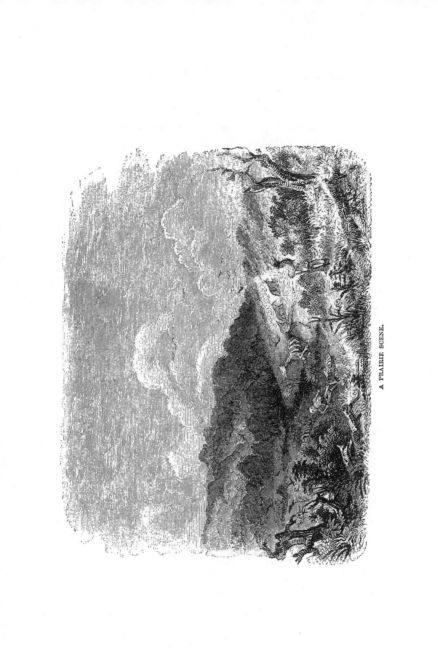

A PRAIRIE SCENE.

tions.'' At length all was ready, and the trader, with a few companions and a small but carefully selected *caballada,* set out upon their trip. They rode hard, but the leader outstripped his men, and by the time that Aubrey had reached the ''Crossing of the Arkansas,'' which is generally considered about halfway, he found himself, with his last horse given out, alone, and on foot. Nothing daunted, however, he pushed on, and reached Mann's Fort, some 15 or 20 miles from the ford. Here he procured a remount, and then, without waiting to rest, or scarcely to break his fast, he departed and once more took the trail. Near Pawnee Fork he was pursued, and had a narrow escape from a party of Indians, who followed him to the creek; but finally he entered the village of Independence within less than the time which he himself had specified. It is said that, upon being assisted from the saddle, it was found to be stained with his blood.

Upon the day following the passage of the Arkansas we halted near Mann's Fort, a little government post, or half-way dépôt, then garrisoned by a handful of volunteers, who drank corn whisky, consumed Uncle Sam's bacon and hard tack, drew their pay with undeviating regularity, and otherwise wore out their lives in the service of the country. In the meantime these doughty warriors dispelled their *ennui* by chasing buffalo, or sallying forth to scout up and down, with a general understanding that they were to quarrel with the Comanches if they could catch them—a combination of circumstances which, as it requires two parties to make a bargain, occurred but seldom.

If I recollect rightly, it was in this vicinity that my attention was attracted by the skeletons of so large a number of mules that I was induced to institute some inquiry in regard to them. Upon doing so I learned that a year or two before some unfortunate trader, in endeavoring to make the trip after the cold weather had set in, lost, by freezing, 120 of his *caballada* in a single night—an event which obliged him to leave his wagons, which, as I have understood, were afterward discovered and burned by the savages. Since then it has "become fashionable" with the idle teamsters, while encamped near the spot, to amuse themselves by arranging and re-arranging these disjointed bones into separate heaps. When I last saw them the leg-bones were laid in rows, having been placed with great regularity, while the skulls formed a ghastly circle upon the ground.

CHAPTER X

FROM THE PAWNEE FORK TO INDEPENDENCE

Delayed by a flood—Dead buffaloes—Description of the prairies—Another buffalo hunt—The Indians take a hand—A narrow escape—A dash ahead of the caravan—Arrival at Independence—Death of Old Bill Williams.

IT was late in the afternoon of a sultry day in August when we encamped upon the borders of a stream known as the Pawnee Fork of the Arkansas. When we reached it its waters were at their lowest stage, being scarcely knee-deep at the ford; but our wagon-master concluded not to cross until the ensuing day—a rather unwise procedure in frontier traveling, where the most approved rule is, "Pass a river while you can." In this instance our departure from so prudent a maxim was bitterly regretted by all who felt any anxiety to reach the Settlements. For though the sun set brightly, the deepening twilight brought freshening winds and gloomy clouds, the forerunners of a storm, whose pouring torrents drenched us to the skin, and threatened our devoted camp with a renewal of the deluge upon a small scale. Nor was it until high noon of the following day that the sun peeped out from the misty wrappings to dry our wagon-covers and promise a cessation of the rain. But alas! for our future prospects, the modest stream of yesterday was now a full-grown river, white with eddying bubbles, and so swollen with its new-born importance that it went roaring and blustering along, tossing the driftwood hither and thither, picking noisy quarrels with the gnarled roots of venerable trees, and altogether comporting itself like a mad, headstrong brawler of a torrent as it was. As any attempt to cross it in its then agitated condition was a thing not to be thought of, we resigned ourselves to our ill-fortune with what philosophy we might, and, having located a water-mark, retired to our camp to wait until "something should turn up," or, which would be equally satisfactory under the circumstances, till the waters should go down.

As we would be stationary for that day at least, I tried to while away the time by taking my gun and sallying forth with the hope of killing something which might diversify the monotony of bacon and hard bread. With this praiseworthy desire I walked down the river, following the windings of the stream until having gained a sufficient offing from our fires, when I left it abruptly, intending to make a considerable detour, and then return to the water at some point yet lower down. So far as game was concerned, this tramp of mine proved anything but a successful one; for, save a prowling wolf and a dismal-featured owl, I regained the river without en-

PAINTED TREES.

countering anything which would justify the expenditure of a cartridge. Upon once more nearing its banks I remarked a strong and almost overpowering stench, which grew more terrible as I advanced. Curious to discover the cause I pushed on, the expostulations of my olfactories to the contrary notwithstanding, and found the swollen stream to be literally filled with the bloated and putrid carcasses of decaying buffalo. They had been driven, most probably, by Indians into the swampy lands adjoining this portion of the Fork, where they had mired down by hundreds.

It was truly a revolting spectacle, and I soon felt anxious to escape from the dreadfully sickening air; so turning my back upon the tainted stream, I followed, as nearly as the denseness of the undergrowth would permit, the general direction of the river, until I caught sight of our white wagon-covers, and once more regained the camp. Before doing so, while passing a thicket in the river-bottom, I found a little grove of trees, the trunks of which had been partially barked and rudely painted with Indian hieroglyphics, the interpretation whereof was doubtless best known to their authors—at all events, *I* didn't care, after my recent adventure upon the Arkansas, to spend much time in deciphering them, the more so as it was by no means improbable that their authors might drop in unexpectedly to interfere with my studies. At our "Water Camp," as we called this enforced halting-place, we were doomed to spend the two succeeding days; and then —the waters having receded sufficiently to permit of our departure—we went on our way rejoicing, determined that henceforth our camp should be upon the right side of a creek, and, if possible, a little beyond it.

And now, as we have accomplished more than half our journey, it may not be out of place to introduce at this point of our narrative such brief remarks as the limits of an article will permit upon the general features, climate, and animal life of the Great Prairies.

The most fertile district of the plains lies east of the Diamond Spring. The soil is here better adapted to cultivation, the grasses more luxuriant, and the flowers of a gayer dye than upon any other portion of the trail. There is also a marked difference in the quality of the timber that fringes the streams or unites to form the beautiful groves which charm the eye of the *voyageur* as he approaches the waters of the Missouri, and that which is found between Diamond Spring and the settlements of New Mexico. Indeed as the cotton-wood is almost the only tree which is met with until you reach Council Grove, and not even that unless upon the banks of some never-failing river, where it is protected from the fires which sweep annually the surrounding country, the traveler is necessarily obliged to depend for his *fuel* upon the dried buffalo dung, which furnishes an excellent substitute for wood for all culinary purposes. As regards the supply of *water* (putting its quality out of the question, for of that I can say but little which is favorable), the traveler will never be put to serious inconvenience—except, perhaps, upon the Cimarron, or between that river and the crossing of the Arkansas. Indeed, in our own case, we suffered more from a superabundance than a scarcity.

The climate of the "Great Prairies" is excellent. I never enjoyed better health than while traversing them; and I would cordially recommend any person who is suffering from dyspepsia or a tendency to consumption to pack up his traps, take leave of the doctor, and "throw physic to the dogs," or out of the window if he prefers it, and then, with a good horse and one of Sharpe's patent rifles, a bowie-knife, and a Colt's six-shooter, let him "make a break" and go westward to the spurs of the Rocky Mountains; and, believe me, if living in the open air, rough fare, and rougher exercise—and, above all, the pure atmosphere of this elevated region—do not work wonders and effect a cure the case must be an uncommon one and bad indeed.

Among the numerous animals who find their homes or feeding-grounds in this remote region, we may enumerate the following: The buffalo; elk; antelope; mustang, or wild horse; prairie wolf, or *coyote* (*canis latrans*); the large gray wolf; and, in the vicinity of timber, the black bear; while *least,* but seldom *last* upon the list, the little *prairie dog* claims his share of attention.

The buffalo, the universal theme of prairie travelers, are to be found at times in such immense herds that their huge forms darken the plain as far as the eye can reach, while the very earth seems trembling beneath the shock of their trampling hoofs, as they rend the air with deep-mouthed bellowings. The habits of this animal would appear to be marked with a certain regularity. For instance, they usually spend the day—unless in intensely hot weather—in feeding along the ridges, where the watchful bulls draw a *cordon,* as it were, of sentinels about the herd, and, thanks to their sensitive noses! give instant warning of the approach of danger if coming from the windward. In the morning and at sundown they generally leave their feeding pastures to seek the pools, often many miles distant, from whence they drink. In migrating for this purpose the buffalo commonly follow each other in Indian file; thus forming those innumerable paths, or "buffalo trails," as they are called, which traverse almost every portion of their feeding-grounds. Occasionally the leading bull will halt to roll himself upon the grass (most probably to clear the hide from dust or vermin). Upon reaching the same spot the next buffalo will follow his example; and so on throughout the herd. This accounts for the holes, or "buffalo wallows," as they are styled, which are so frequently to be met with upon the Great Prairies. There are two modes of hunting this animal—on horseback and upon foot. The former method, which is much the most exciting, is that usually resorted to by the savages, of whose exploits in this way a prairie writer speaks as follows:

"The Indians as well as Mexicans hunt the buffalo mostly with the bow and arrows. For this purpose they train their fleetest horses to run close beside him, and when near enough, with almost unerring aim they pierce him with their arrows, usually behind the short ribs ranging forward, which soon disables and brings him to the ground. When an arrow has been mis-directed, or does not enter deep enough, and even when it has penetrated a vital part but is needed to use again, the hunter sometimes rides up and draws it out while the animal is yet running. An athletic Indian will not unfrequently discharge his darts with such force that I have seen them (30 inches long) wholly buried in the body of a buffalo; and I have been assured by hunters that the arrows, missing the bones, have been known to pass entirely through the huge carcass and fall upon the ground."

The method of hunting upon foot—or "still hunt-ing," as it is termed—requires a greater amount of caution, and is infinitely more laborious than the chase upon horseback. In the one case you have only to urge on your steed, taking care to keep him so perfectly under your control that you may be en-abled to jump him aside at a moment's warning, in case the enraged beast should (as it is apt to do when too closely pressed) make a rush at you with his dangerous horns; but in "still hunting" the thing is managed differently. In this instance the hunter must take advantage of every favorable peculiarity of the ground as he crawls cautiously upon his prey; and, above all, he must keep himself carefully to leeward of his prey; for should the buffalo "wind" him, even though he may have been as yet unseen, the alarmed animal will carry his hump steaks far beyond the reach of even a Jake Hawkins rifle in double-quick time. In buffalo shooting it is useless to throw away your ammunition by aiming at the head; you might as well expend your balls upon a stone-wall outright, as to imagine that they would pierce the thickness of skull and matted hair which protects the brain of a full-grown buffalo bull. After all I prefer the "still hunting," for if you be cool and wary you may crawl upon a herd, and after dropping one of the bulls "on post," creep up and, by making a barricade of his huge body, secure as many of the beasts as you may require.

So much for the "monarch of the plains"; and now for a description of the least among their four-legged inhabitants—the little "prairie dog," which has been called, and probably is, a species of marmot. This diminutive animal has attracted the notice and elicited a "favorable mention" from almost every prairie writer. Among others, Gregg alludes to it in the following strain:

PRAIRIE DOG VILLAGE.

"Of all the prairie animals by far the most curious, and by no means the least celebrated, is the little prairie dog. This singular quadruped is not much larger than the common squirrel, its body being nearly a foot long, with a tail of three or four inches. The color ranges from brown to a dirty yellow. Its flesh, though often eaten by travelers, is not esteemed savory. Its yelp, which seems its only canine attribute, resembles that of the little toy-dog. A collection of their burrows is usually termed a 'dog-town,' which comprises from a dozen or so to some thousands in the same vicinity, often covering an area of many thousand square feet. They generally locate upon firm dry plains, coated with fine short grass, upon which they feed, for they are no . doubt exclusively herbivorous. But even when tall coarse grass surrounds they seem commonly to destroy this within their 'streets,' which are nearly always found paved with a fine species suited to their palates. They must need but little water, if any at all, as their 'towns' are often, indeed generally, found in the midst of the most arid plains—unless we suppose that they dig down to subterranean fountains. At least they evidently burrow remarkably deep. Attempts to dig or drown them out of their holes have commonly proved unsuccessful."

For myself I could never bear to interfere with the gambols of these playful little creatures by shooting at them. They seemed such "jolly dogs," and had such a comical, good-natured way about them, that I derived a much greater pleasure in watching their pranks than I could have gained from "making *game*" of them. I liked to come suddenly upon their "towns," and watch the precipitation with which some villager who had been caught too far from home would retreat to the nearest burrow. How quickly he would make his short legs fly, and what a comical figure he would cut in scampering across the ground; but once at his own door, how resolutely the little rascal would face about and raise himself, squirrel-like, upon his hind-legs, to shake his head and utter a sharp, irritated yelp, ere he precipitated himself, head-foremost, into the cellar of his under-ground habitation. It is an old saying, that "poverty makes strange bed-fellows"; and I fancy that the poor prairie dogs lead rather a hard life of it at times, from the society which is forced upon them; for besides the "dogs" and their infant families, you will find each burrow inhabited by a rattlesnake and a small owl. Whether these last-named inmates take "possession," and are thenceforth deaf to all "notices to quit," or whether they are a kind of country cousin on a summer visit to the houses of their four-footed friends it is impossible to say. They would appear to get along amicably together, but I am inclined to believe that the younger pups sometimes find the presence of these "boarders" a very *killing* sort of nuisance.

We had just completed one of our shortest day's travel; certain moving objects in the distance revived my buffalo fever, and awoke, moreover, a longing for "hump steaks." So I set out alone from camp. When I reached the river I found that the buffaloes were on the opposite side; and that, moreover, they were making off with all their ungainly speed. One old bull, however, lagged behind; and I resolved to give him a trial at all events. So I forded the shallow river, and thereby nearly came to grief. It would be a long story to tell how I stalked the old veteran, gave him several shots which ought to have killed him, but somehow did not; how I prepared to give him one more, which I was fully persuaded would serve to introduce his huge carcass to a very intimate acquaintance with my hunting-knife.

But that shot was never destined to be fired; for as the rammer clinked in the barrel I beheld what, at first sight, would seem to be a mustang, as the wild horse of the prairies is commonly called, rising the grassy ridge that divided me from the yellow sand-hills. As a mustang is an everyday matter in this section of country, I was not at first disposed to pay any particular attention to its movements. But a moment's consideration assured me that there was something unusual in its appearance, which, coupled with the fact that I was sufficiently versed in hunter's craft to know that the wild horse of the prairies would never willingly advance toward the spot on which I stood, in the very face of the strong wind which was then blowing freshly from my position to his, and which would immediately inform him of my presence, induced me to scan this new-comer more clearly. Ere five minutes had elapsed another, and yet another mustang followed it, and as they came rapidly toward me three Indians, who had hitherto been concealed by lying upon the farther side of their horses, now rose suddenly into a sitting posture upon their saddles, and announced at once their own most undesirable proximity and my imminent peril.

Had I been upon horseback, or had there been a cover to which I might retreat if too closely pressed, I should have felt but little uneasiness; for with a good gun and plenty of ammunition, and a chance to run away if you can't do better, one white man is, or ought to be, equal to two redskins, or possibly, when your scalp depends upon the issue, even three. But situated as I was, on foot and alone, with two long miles between myself and assistance, I must confess that I felt somewhat "hurried." I hardly fancied "a fire in the rear"; but to stop where I was seemed even less desirable. So with one look at my wounded buffalo, I muttered, "I reckon you're no great account after all, hardly worth butchering"; adding, as the new arrivals took a direction which might head me off from the river, "Deuce take the

fellow who calls this kind of hunting good sport!''
But there was no time to be lost; so I ''put out''
forthwith, and made what a Kentuckian would have
called ''the tallest kind of tracks'' for water.

Upon reaching the brink of the Arkansas I felt
satisfied that it was not my ford; but as my situation was just at that moment not unlike the gentleman's who, having got into difficulties, was a ''little
pressed for time,'' I ''plunged in, accoutred as I
was.'' Nor did I tarry to ''bid them follow,'' knowing that they would take that liberty without waiting for the ceremony of an invitation. I had barely
floundered, with my musket for company, into a hole
where the water was ''seven feet large,'' the author
being ''six scant,'' when a chorus of yells from the
bank, followed by the dash of an arrow or two into
the water beside me, with the prospect of another
better aimed next time, assured me of the arrival of
my pursuers.

I remember diving and remaining under water
until I concluded that the possibility of being shot
was preferable to the certainty of being drowned
should I remain much longer submerged. But on
coming up to breathe, chuck went another arrow
into the stream, within a most uncomfortable proximity to my devoted head—a procedure which induced me to go under in haste. It would occupy
more space than I could conveniently afford were

I to chronicle all my ups and downs, duckings and divings, ere I finally struck bottom and once more regained the shallow water; and then, in less time than it takes to write it, I "might have been seen" making for a little thicket of reeds which I had observed at the upper extremity of the sand-bar that I was then traversing.

Having reached this cover, which I found sufficiently dense to furnish a temporary concealment, I halted to breathe, and then, in nautical phrase, proceeded to "take an observation." A single glance convinced me that if the Comanches had had it all in their own way at first, they had but little to brag of now. My apparent mishap in getting into deep water had evidently saved me; for the savages, in their hurry to overtake me, had ridden in until their horses had fairly logged down among the treacherous quicksands of the Arkansas, where their disappointed yells, as their steeds floundered helplessly in the mire, gave abundant proof of their anxiety to get forward. As may readily be supposed, I felt anything but sympathy with their misfortunes. Indeed, next to their having broken their necks, I considered it the very best thing which could possibly have happened to them, and only hoped that they might continue to remain fixtures. "My star is in the ascendant at last, and I'll teach you to interfere with my afternoon amusements!" was my

mental exclamation as I slipped a few more buck-
shot down the barrel of my gun, having previously
poured a pint or two of water from the muzzle as
a necessary preparation before using it against the
copperskins.   I then, with no amiable intentions,
got a long, steady aim at Comanche No. 1, who looked
anything but pleased with the selection as he
writhed himself like a wounded snake in the saddle,
at the same time yelping at me most dismally for
want of a more killing mode of annoyance.   Having
cast my eye along the barrel until I was fully satisfied that one at least of my pursuers would be placed
beyond the help of Indian surgery, I pulled trigger,
but only to discover that a wet gun is a poor tool to
fight with.   Having tried two more caps with no
better success, I concluded, as my enemies seemed
to be getting out of their embarrassment, that it
would be best to depart.   And it was well that I did
so; for I had barely left my position when my pursuers extricated themselves from theirs. It was still
rather "a near thing"; for I was on foot, single-
handed and almost unarmed, while they were three
in number, well furnished with weapons, and
mounted upon horses, somewhat tired, it is true, with
their exertions in the river, but still abundantly able
to get over the ground much faster than myself.
Luckily for me, the "river bottom" just at this point
consists of a succession of ridges, well covered at

A SHOT AT THE COMANCHES.

that season of the year with a luxuriant growth of long grass. In this grass I took refuge; and by dint of crawling while ascending a slope, and running when an intervening ridge sheltered me from my pursuers, I managed to elude the Indians, who searched for me upon every side, and would inevitably have overtaken me had not the strong wind which was blowing at the time kept the grass in continual agitation, so as to render it impossible to detect any particular movement in its midst. I finally reached camp about dusk, hungry, tired, wet, and withal as much scared by my adventure as I had ever been before or would willingly be again. It was certainly a narrow escape. Had I been taken my story would have been a brief one: my bones might have furnished matter for speculation to some future traveler, while my curly scalp would have adorned the lodge of a Comanche brave, or, it may be, have been sent as a delicate token of affection to some copper-colored belle of the wilderness by her Indian admirer.

Between the Arkansas and Cottonwood Creek we passed, among other camping-grounds, those of Cow Creek, Little Arkansas, and Turkey Creek, at each of which we lay down and rose again, broke bread and boiled coffee, without meeting with an adventure which might be recorded here. Upon nearing the Cottonwood—a little stream that takes its name from the trees which cast their broad shadows across its placid waters—we overtook a long cavalcade of *friendly* Indians, probably so called from the fact that they are protected by the United States, and display their gratitude by stealing from our citizens whenever an opportunity is afforded them for pilfering with security. These were the Sacs and Foxes, who were then returning from a buffalo hunt upon the Great Prairies. We found these copper-colored gentry in high feather from the successful termination of a recent difficulty with their mortal enemies the Pawnees, with whom they had had a skirmish which resulted in the death of a couple of Pawnee braves, whose scalps, it was reported, were even then journeying toward the Settlements among the household traps and plunder of a Sac chief. These fellows, with their gay blankets, ponies, packs, strange attire, and fantastic equipments, presented quite a picturesque appearance as they followed each other in Indian file across the plain. A drive of eight miles from Cottonwood brought us to Lost Spring, and fifteen more to a clear fountain of sweet cold water whose crystal-like purity has justly won for it the title of the "Diamond Spring." From thence we pressed onward, making our jaded cattle do their best in our anxiety to reach Council Grove, the nearest American settlement.

Upon the afternoon of the day following our departure from Council Grove we encamped for the night in some timber bordering on a stream known as Hundred and Ten Mile Creek. From this point to Independence the distance is estimated at from ninety-five to one hundred miles; and as the road was no longer dangerous, Danvar and myself, impatient of the snail-like progress of the trains, determined to press forward, and by dint of hard riding anticipate the arrival of the caravan at our destination by a couple of days. With this intention we passed the evening in preparing for our contemplated trip by baking a quantity of biscuit in one of those three-legged iron conveniences known to the initiated as a "Dutch bake-oven." To these apologies for the "staff of life" we added some ground coffee, a little brown sugar, and a few slices of cooked bacon, and then, having slung a battered tin coffee-pot with a couple of cups to match to the horn of a saddle, by way of camp-equipage, we lay down to sleep until the first glimmer of the morning should shed its light upon our road.

Daybreak found us in the saddle, and as we departed I turned my head more than once to gaze, with a certain feeling of regret, upon the shadowy forms of the huge wagons with which we had for nearly sixty days been traveling. By nightfall we reached a point of low scrubby timber, or rather undergrowth, known as "Black Jack": here we halted, and after a sort of picnic supper lay down to sleep. The afternoon had been a gloomy one, and the evening's promise of rain had begun to be fulfilled as I rolled myself in my solitary blanket with a saddle for my pillow. But I was by far too weary to mind trifles, and fell asleep in spite of the great drops which came pattering down upon my face as I departed for the "land of Nod." It was after daybreak when I awoke, and upon clearing my eyes from the rain-water, the first object which met my gaze was the lugubrious countenance of my afflicted friend, who, wrapped in the ample folds of a Navajo *serape*—supposed by a popular fiction to be water-proof—was making himself most intensely ridiculous in his desperate attempts to assume such a pyramidical formation as might best enable him to shed water.

After a vain attempt to kindle a fire we opened mess-bags, which were found to contain a moist composite of soaked bread, brown sugar, and bacon, which, with the help of a broken paper of pepper, made up a delightful mess. It was no use grumbling, so we betook ourselves to the saddle, where the first four hours' riding proved—thanks to drenched buckskins and dripping saddle leathers!—anything but agreeable. It cleared by noon, but with the meridian heat of an August sun came a new vexation in the shape of a legion of horse-flies, which buzzed noisily

about the ears of our animals, settling, in spite of
our united efforts, upon every unguarded portion of
their bodies—where they practiced phlebotomy to an
extent that nearly maddened the poor beasts, whose
heated flanks were soon fairly blood-stained from
the number and severity of the bites. We soon found
ourselves obliged to encamp; but as the day waned
the insects disappeared, and at four o'clock in the
afternoon we once more mounted to complete our
final march.

By sundown we had crossed the State line of Missouri, in passing which Danvar declared that, if it
were not for stopping his tired animal, he would
get down and kiss the ground, so delighted was he
to set foot upon the soil of a State that contained
all which was dearest to him—his wife and child.
Though my friend had the advantage of me in these
respects, I sympathized most fully with his enthusiasm; so we celebrated the event by giving three
hearty cheers, and then pushed ahead. We rode
hard, making our jaded horses do their best, and
entered the thriving village of Independence at two
o'clock A.M. of the ensuing day.

I was up betimes, for when the brain is busy it
is no easy matter for the body to sleep. What an
astonishing thing a four-post bedstead was; how
very large a two-story brick house looked! I seemed
walking in a dream. How pleasant it was to sit down

once more to "corn doins and chicken fixens"; and
how exceedingly embarrassing under such circumstances to be hampered with such conveniences as
forks, cups, spoons, and all the various et ceteras
without which civilized humanity is unable to feed
itself! But with these minor draw-backs we enjoyed high physical health and wonderful appetites,
and withal a feeling of self-reliance, which inspired
us with a consciousness of superior power; for we
had breathed the pure atmosphere of the Great
Prairies until every nerve was braced, and every
sinew strengthened to its fullest vigor.

My story is told. From the broad Bay of San
Francisco to the turbid waters of the rapid Missouri,
I have laid before the reader the incidents of my
journey; but kind recollections of the rough yet true
souled men who were my companions, ay, and
friends also, during this adventurous trip, have been
revived in their preparations for the press, and I
should do my own heart injustice if I neglected to
pay the tribute of a few remarks to those who have
warmed themselves by my camp fire and slumbered
beside my bed. Frémont has written most truth-
fully when he says, in referring to the strength of
this sympathy, that "men who have gone through
such dangers and sufferings as we had seen become
like brothers, and feel each other's loss; to defend
and avenge each other is the deep feeling of all."

The existence of these hardy mountaineers is one of continual peril and privation. Its rewards are vigorous health and strong excitement. Its end, in most cases, a violent death and an unknown grave; or, haply, a broken arrow, a shivered lance, and the disjointed fragments of a bleaching skeleton lie scattered upon the prairie, the sole relics left by the wolf and vulture to chronicle the fate of one who struggled until numbers overcame the resistance of despair.

I have spoken of the oftentimes violent termination of the mountain man's career. I will conclude by quoting from the pages of *Ruxton's Life in the Far West* his description of the tragic end of a trapper, one of whose adventures I narrated in my "Ride with Kit Carson." He says:

"During the past winter a party of mountaineers, flying from overpowering numbers of hostile Sioux, found themselves, one stormy evening, in a wild and dismal cañon near the elevated mountain valley called the 'New Park.'

"The rocky bed of a dry mountain torrent, whose waters were now locked up at their spring heads by icy fetters, was the only road up which they could make their difficult way; for the rugged sides of the gorge rose precipitously from the creek, scarcely affording a foothold to even the active Big Horn which occasionally looked down upon the travelers from the lofty summit. Logs of pine, uprooted by the hurri-

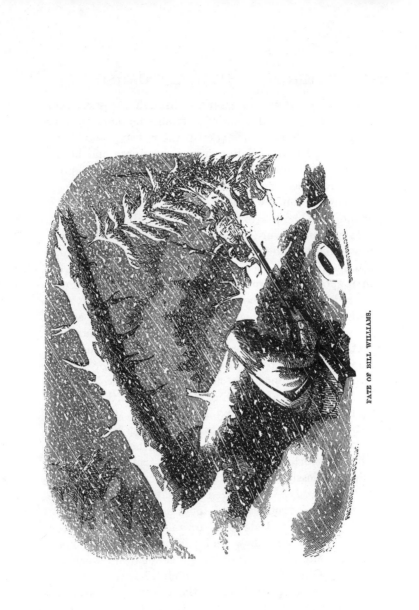

FATE OF BILL WILLIAMS.

canes which sweep incessantly through the mountain
defiles, and tossed headlong from the surrounding
ridges, continually obstructed their way, and huge
rocks and boulders, fallen from the heights and block-
ing up the bed of the stream, added to the difficulty,
and threatened them every instant with destruction.

"Toward sundown they reached a point where the
cañon opened out into a little shelving glade or prairie,
a few hundred yards in extent, the entrance to which
was almost hidden by a thicket of dwarf pine and
cedar. Here they determined to encamp for the night,
in a spot secure from Indians, and as they imagined
untrodden by the foot of man. What, however, was
their astonishment, on breaking through the cedar-
covered entrance, to perceive a solitary horse standing
motionless in the centre of the prairie! Drawing near
they found it to be an old grizzled mustang, or Indian
pony, with cropped ears and ragged tail (well picked
by hungry mules), standing doubled up with the cold,
and at the very last gasp from extreme old age and
weakness. Its bones were nearly through the stiffened
skin, the legs of the animal were gathered under it,
while its forlorn-looking head and stretched-out neck
hung listlessly downward, almost overbalancing its
tottering body. The glazed and sunken eye, the protruding and froth-covered tongue, the heaving flank
and quivering tail, declared its race was run; and the
driving sleet and snow and penetrating winter blast
scarce made impression upon its callous and worn-out
frame. One of the band of mountaineers was Mar-
cellin, and a single look at the miserable beast was
sufficient for him to recognize the once renowned Nez-

percé steed of old Bill Williams. That the owner himself was not far distant he felt certain, and searching
carefully around the hunters presently came upon an
old camp, before which lay, protruding from the snow,
the blackened remains of pine logs. Before these which
had been the fire, and leaning with his back against a
pine trunk, and his legs crossed under him, half-
covered with snow, reclined the figure of the old mountaineer, his snow-capped head bent over his breast. His
well-known hunting-shirt, of fringed elk-skin, hung
stiff and weather-stained about him; and his rifle,
packs, and traps were strewed around.

"Awe-struck, the trappers approached the body, and
found it frozen hard as stone, in which state it had
probably lain there for many days or weeks. A jagged
rent in the breast of his leather coat, and dark stains
about it, showed he had received a wound before his
death; but it was impossible to say whether to his hurt,
or to sickness, or to the natural decay of age, was to
be attributed the wretched and solitary end of poor
Bill Williams.

"A friendly bullet cut short the few remaining hours
of the trapper's faithful steed; and burying as well as
they were able the body of the old mountaineer, the
hunters next day left him in his lonely grave, in a spot
so wild and remote that it was doubtful whether even
hungry wolves would discover and disinter his attenuated corpse."[12]

NOTES

[1] This was apparently Doctor Richard S. Den, an American physician who had come to California in 1843 and was a resident of Los Angeles.

[2] This is not the true Jornado del Muerto, which is in New Mexico. The country now being traversed is, however, sufficiently desolate to merit the name.

[3] Carson, in the dictated story of his life which he gave to Doctor Peters (later expanded into the Peters *Life*), refers to this incident as follows:

"I reached Grand River without any serious difficulty. Then, the river being high, I lost in rafting it, one raft which had on it six rifles and a number of riding and pack saddles. Lieutenant Brewerton was with me. It was near sundown when the raft was lost. Some of the men were on the opposite bank, the Lieutenant among the number. They were nearly naked, had to remain in that situation during the night and in the morning I sent a man over to them with an axe so that they could make another raft. They after some labor, made one and crossed. We then continued our march. Some of the men having to ride bareback until we arrived at Taos."

[4] Brewerton has here managed to be seriously mistaken. That the disaster to the raft on the Grand River actually occurred there, as he says, is confirmed by the independent account by Carson. But going east, as he was, he must have crossed the Green River before he did the Grand. So he must have confused the order of the crossings, remembered that the crossing of the Green was safely accom-

plished, and have come to a false conclusion, plausible enough if based on facts, that a prior dangerous experience had given the skill to avoid a second upset.

[5] Carson, in his dictated story, relates this as follows:

"About fifty miles of Taos we met several hundred Utah and Apache Indians. They showed demonstrations of hostility. We retired into the brush, would only allow a few of them to approach us, informed them that if they were friends, that they should leave, that we were in a naked and destitute condition and could give them nothing. They evidently left us when they saw we had nothing.

"That night I moved on about ten miles and met a party of volunteers on their pursuit of the Apaches."

[6] Though I give this place the name by which it is generally known among the Americans in that section of country, it is geographically incorrect, there being, in reality, no such town. The appellation of *"Taos"* refers more particularly to the *"Valle de Taos,"* so called in honor of the *"Taosa"* tribe of Indians; the remnant of which (as stated by Gregg) yet form a *"pueblo"* in the northern part of the *"valle."* In this, the most beautiful district of New Mexico, are situated several towns and minor settlements, of which Fernandez and Los Ranchos are the most important. (Note by Brewerton.)

[7] The nickname "Greaser" is very generally applied to Mexicans by the Americans residing in our "new acquisitions." It is almost needless to remark that it is no complimentary phrase, being intended as a set-off to the "Gringo"—plain English, greenhorn—by which they are accustomed to designate us. (Note by Brewerton.)

[8] Carson's route as given by himself in his dictated story is:

"Keeping north of the Comanche range, I reached Bijoux, a tributary of the Platte, down it to within twenty-five miles of the South Fork of the Platte, left the Bijoux River and struck for the Platte, kept down it to Fort Kearney, then struck for the Republican Fork and from thence to Fort Leavenworth, having no trouble on the march. Thence to Washington and delivered my dispatches. Returned to St. Louis, remained a few days and started back for New Mexico. Arrived there in October, 1848."

[9] This is the section of the manuscript lost during the fire in Harper's and when finally recovered was printed ten years after the original installments.

[10] It is no uncommon thing for not only buffalo, but even the *caballadas* of the traders, to "stampede," or fly before the heavy gales which sweep the bosom of the Great Prairies. This is particularly the case when, at times, these tempests are accompanied by hail, to escape which the buffalo, when in a wooded country, invariably make for the timbers, even though it should be far distant from their feeding-ground. (Note by Brewerton.)

[11] Francis Xavier Aubry, as the name should be spelled, was a well-known plainsman and trader. He later was an explorer of Arizona. This is believed to be the first account of his ride, which afterward became famous.

[12] This account is purely fanciful, and is one of several inaccurate versions extant. The facts have only recently come to light in the manuscripts, chiefly by Lieutenant Edward Kern, known as *The Fort Sutter Papers*, now in the Huntington Library.

Frémont, this time without Carson, entered the Rocky Mountains in New Mexico in the month of November, 1848, with thirty-one men, on his disastrous fourth expedition.

He was seeking a new route across the continent. Among his party were Williams and the three Kern brothers; Lieutenant Edward Kern, who had been in command at Fort Sutter during the Bear Flag days, R. H. Kern, the artist who made the drawings of the Navajo Indians reproduced in the text, and Dr. Benjamin Kern.

Disregarding the warnings of Williams, who spoke with the knowledge and authority of twenty years in these mountains, Frémont insisted on taking a route that was impracticable. After terrible hardships in the bitter cold and deep snow, which cost the lives of ten men, the survivors reached Taos. Frémont accused Williams of responsibility for the disaster. The Kerns so resented this that they refused to continue with Frémont, and they and Williams quit the expedition.

Lieutenant Kern had been forced to abandon in the mountain passes his records which he rightly considered historically valuable, since they related to his command in 1846-1847. In the spring of 1849, Dr. Kern and Old Bill Williams returned to the place of the abandonment of the documents in order to recover them, and both lost their lives in the attempt, being killed by the Indians.

Additional details are furnished by William T. Hamilton, the famous plainsman. In his *My Sixty Years on the Plains* he says he knew Williams well, having begun his friendship on a journey by wagon train with him as early as 1842, and continued with him for three years. He says (p. 196), ''I never saw Williams again. A few years afterwards the Southern Utes killed him by mistake in Apache Pass. They were great friends of Old Bill, and they packed him to their village and gave him a chief's burial, mourning for him as for one of their own. The Utes themselves told me this.''

BIBLIOGRAPHY

Adventures in Mexico and the Rocky Mountains. George F. Ruxton.

American Fur Trade. H. M. Chittenden.

Annals of San Francisco. Soule, Gihon and Nesbit.

Bigler, Diary of Henry W. *Overland Monthly,* September, 1887.

California, History of. H. H. Bancroft.

California, History of. Josiah Royce.

California under Spain and Mexico. I. B. Richman.

Californian, San Francisco (newspaper). March 15, 1848.

Californias, Pictorial Travels in the. T. J. Farnham.

Canadiens de L'Ouest. Joseph Tasse.

Capitol, Washington, D. C. (newspaper). May 29, 1875.

Carson, Kit, in California. Charles L. Camp.

Carson, Own Story. Blanche C. Grant.

Carson, Life of Kit. Dewitt C. Peters.

Carson Days. E. L. Sabin.

Carson, Life of Kit. Charles Burdett.

Carson. Stanley Vestal.

Catholic Church in Utah. W. R. Harris.

Central Route to the Pacific. Gwinn Harris Heap.

Clyman, James. Charles L. Camp.

Colorado River, Romance of. F. S. Dellenbaugh.

Commerce of the Prairies. Josiah Gregg.

Death Valley in 1849. W. L. Manley.

Doniphan's Expedition. J. T. Hughes.

Eagle, Brooklyn (newspaper). February 1, 1901.
293

Exploring Expedition to the Rocky Mountains.   J. C. Frémont.

Forty-Niners. Stewart Edward White.

Fort Sutter Papers (manuscript). Huntington Library.

Frémont, Memoirs of My Life. J. C. Frémont.

Frémont, Memoir of. John Bigelow.

Frémont and the Forty-Niners. J. C. Dellenbaugh.

Garces' Diary. Elliott Coues.

Hamblin, Jacob. J. A. Little.

Herald, New York (newspaper). Aug. 16, 1848; Sept. 6, 1848; Oct. 10, 1848; Nov. 13, 1848; Nov. 30, 1848; Dec. 26, 1848.

Hollingsworth, Journal of J. H.

Life in the Far West. George F. Ruxton.

Mormons. John W. Gunnison.

Mormon Battalion. Daniel Tyler.

My Sixty Years on the Plains. W. T. Hamilton.

Nevada, Colorado and Wyoming, History of. H. H. Bancroft.

New Mexico, Leading Facts. R. E. Twitchell.

Pacific Railway Reports. Beckwith and Others.

Pattie, Personal Narrative of James C.

Polk, Diary of James C. Ed. M. F. Quaife.

Rough Times and Rough Places. Micajah McGehee, Century Magazine, March, 1891.

Sante Fé Trail. U. S. Geological Survey, 1916.

Santa Fé Trail. Inman and Cody.

Sherman, W. T., Memoirs of.

Sherman, W. T., Home Letters of.

Six Months in the Gold Fields. E. S. Buffum.

Smith-Ashley Explorations. H. C. Dale.

Stevenson's Regiment. Francis D. Clark.

Sun, New York (newspaper). Feb. 2, 1901.
Taos Trail. L. H. Garrard.
Tour in Northern Mexico. A. Wislezenus.
Utah, History of. H. H. Bancroft.

INDEX

Abiquiu, 10, 12.
Agawa Plateau, 8.
Agua de Hernandez, 93.
Agua de Tomaso, 89.
Alcalde Guerrara, 164.
American Fork, 14.
Annsville, 26.
Apache Indians, 290.
Apache Pass, 292.
Archambeau, 96, 115.
Archillette, 87.
Arizona, 5.
Arkansas Crossing, 258.
Arkansas River, 250, 264, 274.
Aubry, 252, ride of, 254, 291.
Aztec ruins, 203.

Barrington, ship, 31.
Beale, 212.
Bear Creek, 10.
Bear flag, 292.
Beaver Dam Range, 7.
Beaver, town of, 8.
Beckwith, report cited, 9.
Benton, 212.
Big-horn, 110, 126, 242, 284.
Bigler, diary quoted, 17.
Bijoux River, 291.
Boon's Lick, 92.
Brackett, Captain, 24.
Brewerton, Caroline Louise Knight, 23.
Brewerton, G. D., birth and parentage, 23; entered army, 24; sailed on Loo Choo, 24; service in California, 24; ordered East, 25; service in Regular Army, 25; literary work, 25, 26; landscape artist, 26; later life and death, 27.

Brewerton, Henry, 23.
Brewerton, Journey of, meets Carson, 37; outfit, 39, 49; camp at Bridge Creek, 41; start, 47; composition of party, 49; lost in desert, 72; visit by Diggers, 75; meets Walker, 77; trails Digger, 96; arrives Las Vegas de Santa Clara, 97; meets Wacarra, 100; at Little Salt Lake, 104; horse trade, 104; in Wasatch Mountains, 108; at Grand (Green) River, 113; loss of stores, 120; hunger, 123; tries buy dog, 125; at Continental Divide, 130; meets Mexican traders, 135; meets hostile Indians, 136; reaches New Mexican huts, 141; reaches Taos, 143; leaves Carson at Taos, 153; shot at, 154; entertained by Father Ignatio, 158; arrives Santa Fé, 176; seeing the elephant, 185; has influenza, 200; Carson leaves alone, 200; start with traders, 201; on Santa Fé Trail, 201, 227 et seq.; buffalo hunt, 235; meets Aubry, 252; fight with Comanche, 272; arrives Independence, 282.
Bridge Creek, 39.
Bridger, Fort, 5.
Brooklyn, 26.
Bucephalus, 202, 234, 251.
Buffalo, hunt, 235, 266; stampede, 247; carcasses of drowned, 262; as food, 253; habits, 266.
Byron, 61.

Cajon Pass, 7.
Californian, newspaper, first publication of gold discovery, 13.
Cape Horn, 20.
Caravan, Mexican, description, 224; 6, 58, 100, 135.
Carson, 3, 8, 9; on Uinta, 11, 12; news of gold, 13; brings mail, 15; guide to Frémont and Kearney, 22, 36; description of, 37; habits on march, 65 et seq.; avenges Mexicans, 89; reports Tabeau missing, 94; misses Digger, 97; builds raft, 114; on deer hunt, 128; withstands Indians, 136; home and wife in Taos, 143; Indian agent, 143; arrives Santa Fé, 200; leaves for Leavenworth, 200; route, 290; quoted on disaster at Grand River, 289.
Castle Dale, 8, 10.
Chama River, 6, 10, 12.
Chittenden, map cited, 9.
Chouteau, 19.
Cimarron jornada, 250.
Cimarron River, 242, 250, 264.
Cimarron Route, 12.
Clark, Fort, 25.
Cochetope Pass, 11.
Cold Spring, 242.
Colorado River (of West), 6, 8; see also Grand River.
Colorado, River (of New Mexico), 227.
Colorado, State, 10, 12.
Columbus, Fort, 24.
Comanche Indians, 220, 228, 251, 259, 275.
Comanche Range, 29, 291.
Continental Divide, 10, 11, 130.
Cottonwood Creek, 10, 278.
Council Grove, 254, 279.
Cow Creek, 278.
Crosses, roadside, 155.
Crossing of Arkansas, 258.
Crossing of Fathers, 6.

Dana, R. H., 123.
Danvar, 233, 280.
D., Doctor; see Den.
Den, Doctor, 33, 289.
Denver & Rio Grande R. R., 9.
Desert travel, 64.
Diamond Spring, 264, 279.
Digger Indians, 63, 74, 75 et seq., 84, 96; see also Eutaw Indians.
Dolores River, 6, 10.
Durango, 10.

Eagle, newspaper, 26.
Emery; quoted, 203.
Ephraim, 8.
Escalante, Father, 5.
Estofa, 204.
Eutaw Indians, 63, 74, 75, 76, 84, 100, 110, 113, 120, 227, 289.

Fernandez, 290.
Ferron Creek, 10.
Fillmore, 9.
Fires of Montezuma, 204.
Fishing with arrows, 110.
Fish Lake, 8, 11.
Fish Lake Mountains, 8.
Fitzpatrick, 95.
Fordham, 27.
Folsom, 14.
Fort Bridger, 5.
Fort Columbus, 24.
Fort Clark, 25.
Fort Kearney, 291.
Fort Leavenworth, 16, 200, 291.
Fort Sutter, 292.
Fort Sutter papers, cited, 291.
Forty-Niners, route of, 22.
Franciscans, 4, 5, 6.
Frémont, 3, 8; report cited, 9, 22, 38, 63; quoted, 87; quoted, 94, 212; quoted, 283; and Old Bill Williams, 291.
Fuentes, 87.

Gambling in Santa Fé, 185.
Garces, Father, 5.

Garcia, 45.
Giacome, 88, 92.
Gila River, 5.
Godey, 89, 92.
Gold discovery, 13 et seq., date of, 17.
Grand (Colorado) River, 6, 11, 113, 140; confusion with Green, 289.
Graveyard Corral, 232.
Great Basin, 8, 212.
Great Desert, 53.
Great Pass, 39, 51.
Great Salt Lake, 8.
Gregg, quoted, 190, 195, 268; cited, 208, 290.
Green River, 6, 8, 10; confusion with Grand, 280.
Guerrara, Alcalde, 164.
Gunnison Expedition, 9.
Gunnison River, 11.
Gunnison Valley, 8, 10, 11.

Hamilton, W. T., quoted, 292.
Harper's Magazine, 3.
Hawthorne, Julian, 26.
Herald, newspaper, 14.
Hernandez, Pablo, 87, 92, 93.
Hernandez Spring, 93.
Hollingsworth, 16.
Horse meat, 123.
Hundred and Ten Mile Creek, 280.

Ignatio, Father, 157.
Independence, 3, 16, 219, 254, 258, 282.
Interior Basin, 8, 212.

Jamaica, 21.
Jornada, del Muerto, 69, 289; of Cimarron, 250.

Kearny, 5, 22.
Kern, Benjamin, 292.
Kern, Edward, 291.
Kern, R. H., 198, 292.

Las Vegas de Santa Clara, 7, 98.
La Tules, 189, 234.
Lecompton, 25.
Lewis, 96; shoots Digger, 97.
Little Arkansas, 278.
Little Gray, 165 et seq.
Little Salt Lake, 7, 8, 10, 100, 104.
Loeser, Lieutenant, 20.
Loo Choo, ship, 24.
Los Angeles, 3, 5, 7, 15, 33; description of, 36, 58, 88.
Los Ranchos, 290.
Lost Spring, 234, 279.

Mail, brought East by Brewerton, 15; difficulties of communication, 20.
Malbone, 23.
Mann's Fort, 258.
Marshall, discovery of gold by, 16.
Mason, Colonel, 16; report on gold, 18, 25.
Meek, journey of, 19.
Mexican traders, 6, 68, 135.
Mexican War, 3.
Mexico, treaty of peace, 20, 21.
Middle Spring, 242.
Mirage, 209.
Missouri River, 19.
Mississippi River, 250.
Moab, 10, 11.
Mojave Desert, 5, 6, 7, 39, 53.
Mojave River, 6.
Monero, 12.
Monroe, 24.
Monterey, 31.
Montezuma, fires of, 204.
Mora, 207, 219.
Mormons, settlements in Utah, 10; party of, goes East, 19.
Mountain Meadows, 7.
Muddy Creek, 10.

Navajo Indians, 198.
Nigger Bill, 207, 241, 251.
Nephi, 8.

Nevada, 7.
New Helvetia, 14, 15.
New Mexico, 10, 12.
New Orleans, 21.
New Park, 284.
Nez Perce Indians, 286.

Ocate, 227.
Ogden, 4.
Oregon, Meek messenger from, 19.
Oregon Trail, 5.
Owls, 27.

Panama, 21.
Panguitch Lake, 11.
Panguitch Mountains, 8.
Parowan Mountains, 8, 10.
Parowan, town, 8, 9.
Pau-Eutaw Indians. *See* Digger.
Pavant Mountains, 8.
Pawnee Fork, 258, 260.
Pawnee Indians, 279.
Pecos, 203.
Penole, 46.
Peters, 289.
Pinos Creek, 12.
Platte River, 291.
Point of Rocks, 227.
Point Judith, 34.
Polk, message, 13.
Prairie dogs, 268.
Prairies, described, 221, 264.
Presidio, 24.
Price River, 9, 10.
Punta del Piedras, 227.

Quitchupah Creek, 10.

Rabbitear Creek, 232.
Raft, at Grand River, 114; upset, 120.
Railroad to Pacific, 210.
Rattlesnake, 63, 271; venom, 80.
Republican Fork, 291.
Richman, I. B., cited, 7.
Rio Grande, 10, 11, 12.
Rio Virgen, 94.

Rock Creek, 227, 232.
Round Mound, 232.
Ruxton, quoted, 284.

Sac and Fox Indians, 279.
Sacramento River, 15.
Sahara, 33.
Saint Louis, 15, 16, 256, 291.
Salado, 10.
Salina, Creek, 10.
Salina, town, 8.
Salt Lake, 6.
Salt Lake City, 19.
San Bernardino Mountains, 7.
San Francisco, 1, 9; gold excitement, 14, 15, 31.
San Gabriel, 5, 6, 7.
San Gabriel Mountains, 7.
San Joaquin River, 6.
San Juan River, 6.
San Luis Valley, 11.
San Pedro, 31, 33.
San Rafael River, 10.
Sandy Desert, 39.
Santa Barbara, 31.
Santa Clara Spring, 227.
Santa Fé, 4, 5, 6, 10, 12, 15, 58, 71, 136, 177; described, 195.
Santa Fé Trail, 3, 12, 235, 243, 256.
Saxton, 26.
Scrugham, 25.
Selkirk, 166.
Sevier Lake, 8.
Sevier River, 8, 10.
Sherman, W. T., 15.
Sierra Nevada, 15, 20.
Sioux Indians, 284.
Smith, Jedediah, 4, 6.
Sonoma, 24.
Spanish caravan, 6, 58, 100, 135, 224.
Spanish traders; *see* Mexican traders.
Spanish Fork, 9.
Spanish Trail, 3, 5, 6; course of, 7, 9, 10, 11, 58, 73.
Spanish Valley, 10.

Spindle, Ebenezer, 179.
Standard, newspaper, cited, 19.
Stevenson, Colonel, 24.
Stevenson Regiment, 3.
Storm on prairie, 243.
Sun, newspaper, cited, 19.
Sutter, Captain, 14, 16.
Sutter's Fort, 292.
Sutter's Mill, discovery of gold at, 13, 19.

Tabeau, 94.
Taos, 3, 4, 5, 12, 20; description of, 149, 289; name, 289.
Taos Valley, 31, 290.
Taosa Indians, 290.
Thomas, 138.
Tomaso, Agua de, 89.
Tompkins, 24.
Trout Lake, 11, 111.
Traders, see Mexican traders.
Trappers, 6.
Tules, 189, 234.
Turkey Creek, 278.
Tushar Mountains, 8, 10.

Uinta River, 11.
Uncompahgre River, 11.

United States Hotel, 177.
Upper Spring, 242.
Utah, 5, 6, 7, 8, 19.
Utah Indians, 63, 74, 75, 76, 84, 100, 110, 113, 120, 227, 289.
Utah Lake, 6, 8.
Ute Indians; see Utah Indians.

Virgin River, 6, 94.

Wacarra, 100, 106.
Walker, Joseph, 4, 77.
Wasatch Mountains, 8, 9, 11, 98, 108, 113.
Wasatch Pass, 8, 10.
Washington, 21, 291.
Water Camp, 263.
Weir, R. W., 23.
Williams, Old Bill, horse-stealing expedition, 70; death of, 284, 291.
Wise, quoted, 198.
Wolfskill, 4, 6.
Wouverman, 157.

Yerba Buena, 32.